Painting
on
Glass & Ceramic

Painting
on
Glass & Ceramic

Karen Embry

STERLING

New York / London
www.sterlingpublishing.com

PROLIFIC IMPRESSIONS PRODUCTION STAFF:

Editor in Chief: Mickey Baskett
Copy Editor: Ellen Glass
Graphics: Karen Turpin
Styling: Lenos Key
Photography: Jerry Mucklow
Administration: Jim Baskett

Library of Congress Cataloging-in-Publication Data
Embry, Karen.
   Painting on glass & ceramic / Karen Embry.
      p. cm.
   Includes index.
   ISBN-13: 978-1-4027-5264-3
   ISBN-10: 1-4027-5264-4
   1. Painting--Technique. 2. Glass painting and staining. 3. China painting--Technique. I. Title.

TT385.E48 2008
748.5028'2--dc22
                                                    2007031742

2 4 6 8 10 9 7 5 3 1

Published by Sterling Publishing Co., Inc.
387 Park Avenue South, New York, NY 10016
© 2008 by Prolific Impressions, Inc.
Distributed in Canada by Sterling Publishing
c/o Canadian Manda Group, 165 Dufferin Street,
Toronto, Ontario, Canada M6K 3H6
Distributed in the United Kingdom by GMC Distribution Services,
Castle Place, 166 High Street, Lewes, East Sussex, England BN7 1XU
Distributed in Australia by Capricorn Link (Australia) Pty. Ltd.
P.O. Box 704, Windsor, NSW 2756, Australia

Printed in China
All rights reserved

ISBN-13: 978-1-4027-5264-3
ISBN-10: 1-4027-5264-4

For information about custom editions, special sales, premium and corporate purchases, please contact Sterling Special Sales Department at 800-805-5489 or specialsales@sterlingpub.com.

ACKNOWLEDGEMENTS

Thanks to:

For FolkArt® Enamels™ Paints, Enamels™ Mediums, Stencils, Daubers, Spouncers™, Tip Pen™ Set, grout, and grout/painters tape: Plaid Enterprises, Inc., 3225 Westech Drive, Norcross, GA 30092, 1-800-392-8673, www.plaidonline.com

For brushes: Silver Brush Limited, P.O. Box 414, Windsor, NJ 08561-0414, www.silverbrush.com, (609) 443-4909, e-mail: info@silverbrush.com

For wood frames and boxes that hold ceramic tiles: Wood Creations, 1544 Saddle Court, Palm Harbor, FL 34683, (727) 455-5539, e-mail: woodbytom@aol.com

For underglazes, glazes, bisque ceramic pieces, glaze sticks, and underglaze applicator bottle with mosquito nose tip: Off the Wall Ceramics, 2315 E. Fletcher Avenue, Tampa, FL 33612, 813-977-0792, e-mail: OffTheWallTampa@Yahoo.com

For Pebeo Vitrea Glass Paints: Pebeo, www.pebeo.com e-mail: info@pebeo.com

For Liquitex Glossies Enamel Paints: Liquitex Artist Materials, www.liquitex.com, 888-422-7954

For compressed sponges: The Color Wheel Company, P.O. Box 130, Philomath, Oregon 97370-0130, Phone: (541)929-7526, www.colorwheel.com

For bisque pieces - dog or cat food bowl, dog or cat lover sign, and dog or cat frame: Bisque Imports, 888-568-5991

About Karen Howell Embry

Karen Howell Embry is an artist, designer and author who is passionate about her work. From as far back as the early age of six, she recalls her desire to become an artist. To this day, her passion to create has not wavered. Karen attended the University of South Florida and has taught painting for many years. She has authored numerous painting books and nationally published magazine articles. Karen is an ambassador for Plaid Enterprises, Inc. and travels throughout the country demonstrating and teaching. One of her latest ventures was traveling to the Pentagon in Washington, D.C. teaching and working with the employees of the Pentagon and their children for the "Take Your Child to Work Day." Karen's namesake company, "Karen Embry Designs," is currently focused on the licensing industry. Having exhibited at the Surtex Licensing Show in New York, she has created wonderful new partnerships with manufacturers in the licensing industry. In the very near future you will find Karen's newest designs in the home decor and giftware industry.

If you would like to contact Karen with any questions or comments, you may reach her at khecrafts@aol.com and visit her website at karen@karenembry.com.

A Word from Karen Embry

I recently read a saying that mentioned that this life we are living is not a dress rehearsal. This is it. There are no do-overs . . . and how true that is! So I say to you, reach for your dreams, follow your passion, and do it today. I believe that we should not take one single moment of our wonderful lives for granted. Carpe Diem! Life is meant to be AWESOME!

Dedication

I dedicate this book to my family. When all is said and done, they make it all matter. We have laughed together at the good moments, and cried together at the bad times. What is most important of all is that whatever we are doing, we are doing it together.

Special Thanks

To my husband **Chuck** . . . your endless support in all my creative endeavors has helped to make following my dreams possible. Thank you for being there every day, in every way. I love you.

To my daughter **Davi** and my son **Kyle:** You are the greatest kids ever and, as always, I am so proud of the two of you. You are the joy of my life! I love you guys.

To my **Mom and Dad:** Thanks for being just who you are and for helping me to be just who I am. Married 52 years and counting . . . WOW, you are amazing! Love you.

To **Mickey Baskett,** my editor: As always it is a pleasure to work with you. Thank you for everything!

Page 38

Page 20

CONTENTS

- Introduction   8
- **Part I: Using Non-Fired Glass & Ceramic Paint**   9
- Glass & Ceramic Paints   10
- Brushes   12
- Other Tools   13
- Miscellaneous Basic Supplies   14
- Surfaces   15
- Using the Patterns   16
- Painting Definitions & Techniques   17
- Reverse Painting   18
- Sponging   19
- Stenciling/"Purely Paisley" Canister Set   20
- Stamping/"Garden Flowers" Oval Mirror   22
- Dream Ceramic Mug   24
- Bloom Ceramic Mug   26
- Make a Wish Cake Stand & Candy Jar   30
- Love Love Plate   34
- Bunny in the Garden Container   36
- Kiss a Frog Candy Jar   38
- Fruit of the Vine Wine Glasses & Carafe   42

Page 46

- Citrus Delight Pitcher & Glasses   46
- ABC Baby's Food Jars   50
- Welcome Baby Piggy Bank   56
- Basket of Fruit Framed Ceramic Tiles   62
- St. Patrick's Day Lucky Plate   64
- Happy Mother's Day Plate   66
- Butterfly Garden Vase   69
- Happy Father's Day Martini Glasses   72
- Pretty in Blue Vase   74
- Cinco de Mayo Glassware Set   78
- Happily Ever After Frame & Toast Glasses   80
- Fall Holiday Plate   84
- Owl & Moon Candle Holder   86
- Christmas Holiday Plate   88

- **Part II: Using Kiln Fired Glazes**   91
- Glazes   92
- Brushes   94
- Other Tools   94
- Surfaces   95
- Other Supplies   95
- Painting with Glazes   96
- Transferring Designs   96
- Masking   97
- Stenciling   98
- Stamping   99
- Sponging   100
- Sgraffito   101
- Gifty Mugs   102
- Ruffled Ware Table Set   106
- Trinket Dish Gifts   108
- Colorful Sgraffito Pear Bowl   112
- Woof Dog Bowl   115
- Woof Photo Frame   118
- Woof Dog Lover Sign   120
- Cat Lover Sign   121
- Meow Cat Bowl   122
- Meow Cat Frame   124
- Metric Conversions   127
- Index   127

Go for the "Wow!" Response

Do you have a free afternoon? Believe it or not, that is enough time to turn a plain-jane glass vase or a ho-hum ceramic mug into a hand-painted gift that sparkles with vivid colors. Plus, a hand painted gift is always the most welcome gift of all — it is much more personal, thoughtful, and creative. In this book, you will learn how to use both non-firing paints as well as kiln-fired ceramic paints.

If you haven't checked recently, you will be surprised to see how many new products for painting on glass and ceramic surfaces have reached your local crafts store. They are easier to use than ever before, come in an array of gorgeous colors, and best of all, they can be baked in your kitchen oven to make those colors durable enough to go through the dishwasher.

When you get ready to try your hand at creating kiln fired ceramics, you can visit one of the "paint your own" pottery shops that are springing up in every town. The shop provides bisque ceramic pieces, glazes, and the kiln for firing; you supply the creativity.

Karen Embry has designed a book full of *Wow!*-inspiring gift ideas that will take you from "I do" to "Welcome, Baby;" from "Make a Wish" to "Ho-Ho-Ho!" You will enjoy painting these patterns

created in Karen's lively illustration style. As an extra bonus, Karen's own complete alphabet patterns are in the book. You can use them to personalize your special gifts.

There are some techniques to master, and some new terms to learn (did you know that "sgraffito" refers to a "scratching" technique?) but Karen's explanations and step-by-step painting demonstrations make learning them a pleasure.

This book is divided into two sections. The first section gives you techniques and projects that use several kinds of non-fired glass and ceramic paints that can be air dried or baked in your home oven. The second section tells you what you need to know to create glazed, kiln fired ceramics. Taking both sections together, you will have the patterns and detailed instructions for creating more than 35 pieces. Once you understand how to use both kinds of surface decoration, you will find that it is easy for you to adapt Karen's patterns to fit different pieces using different paints, glazes, and techniques.

As you look through this book, think about your favorite people and the occasions that will arise for giving a gift that will express your affection for them. And think also about how much pleasure *you* will receive from creating these glass and ceramic gifts.

PART I

Using Non-Fired Glass & Ceramic Paints

Paint the projects in this section of the book with opaque or transparent paints, then bake them in an ordinary kitchen oven for colorful, durable effects. With so many products available for painting on glass and ceramic surfaces, how do you choose which one is right for your project? Begin by considering the surface, the effect of the paint, and the durability needed for the use of the piece.

Glass paints come in both opaque and transparent formulations. Opaque paints give a solid-color, painted effect and do not allow light to pass through. Transparent paints come in brilliant colors that give the effect of stained glass, or in frosted shades that mimic the subtlety of etched glass.

If your piece is for decorative use only, air-dried paints will work well. If it will be used and cleaned frequently-a glass, pitcher, plate, or mug-paints that can be baked are more durable. Many can even go through the dishwasher.

Most brands offer a good range of colors, and all glass paints can be easily applied with a brush, dabbed on with a sponge, stamped, or stenciled. Read the manufacturer's specific directions for how to prepare the surface, clean the finished item, and, if necessary, how to seal the painted design.

Food Safety

I have tried most of the non-fired glass and ceramic paints on the market. I have discovered that only one of them is food safe. "Food safe" means you can eat food or drink beverages from the painted surface of a plate, cup, or other container. So please, for your own safety, **read all of the manufacturer's directions and specifications** regarding the product you are using and follow them carefully.

Even if the paints are not listed as "food safe" you can still use them to paint on your dinnerware. There are several ways you can safely use your lovely painted pieces. Leave an unpainted area ⅝" to ¾" from the rim of a glass or mug. Paint clear glass plates on the back (reverse painting) to avoid contact with food. You may wish to use a painted plate as a charger, and serve the food on an unpainted plate that can sit on top of the charger.

If you are painting a piece that will be used for decorative purposes only, such as a vase, you don't need to be concerned with the food safety of the paints.

Glass & Ceramic Paints

Acrylic Enamels, Opaque

These opaque, water-based acrylic paints are available in a wide range of colors, are easy to use, and are oven-baked for extra durability. This type of paint is good for sponging or stenciling as well as brush painting. Clean up your brushes, tools, and painting area with soap and water before the paint dries. If you make a mistake while painting, just rub or wash it away. Mistakes discovered after baking can be scraped away with a craft knife. Follow the manufacturer's instructions for drying, curing, and baking in a home oven.

Transparent Glass & Ceramic Paints

These resin-based paints give the effect of stained glass as their intense pigments allow light to pass through. They are available in both glossy and frosted colors. Clean up your brushes, tools, and painting area with soap and water before the paint dries. The paint is removable until the piece is baked; simply wipe off mistakes with a cotton swab dampened with rubbing alcohol or warm water. Follow the manufacturer's instructions for drying, curing, and baking in a home oven.

Using Mediums and Thinners

Use only the mediums and thinners that are formulated to work with the manufacturer's product line. Most paints for glass and ceramics should not be mixed with water as it will decrease the durability of the paints.

Finishing and Baking

Each manufacturer has specific recommendations as to how the paint should be cured. Some paints require a certain amount of drying time before baking. Please read and follow the instructions on the paint label to

achieve the best adhesion and durability of oven-baked painted pieces. The usual instructions for baking will have you place the piece in a cool oven. Heat to the desired temperature, set a timer, and bake for the required time. Turn off the oven and allow the piece to cool to room temperature before removing it from the oven. The temperature settings of domestic ovens are not always reliable. It is recommended that you use an oven thermometer.

Caring for Painted Pieces

You may hand wash your painted pieces with warm water and dish detergent. Do not allow the pieces to soak in water. Many oven-baked painted pieces can be washed in the top rack of a dishwasher; check the paint label to be sure.

Tips

- **Always** check the label for specific instructions.
- Be sure the paints are well shaken or stirred. Some glossy paints should be stirred for 30-60 seconds.
- Keep painted surfaces horizontal if possible until the paint is completely dry.
- Allow paints to dry for the full time specified on the label. Some paints may slide on glass or ceramic surfaces if they have not been properly air-dried before baking.
- Do not thin paints with water. Use the thinning medium that is recommended or that is part of each line of paint.

Palette of Colors

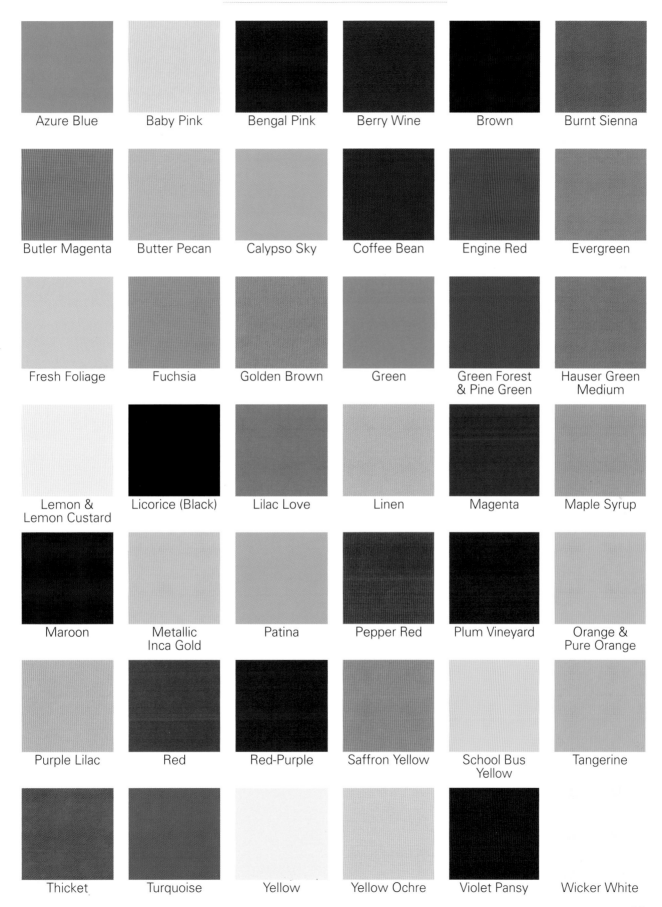

Azure Blue	Baby Pink	Bengal Pink	Berry Wine	Brown	Burnt Sienna
Butler Magenta	Butter Pecan	Calypso Sky	Coffee Bean	Engine Red	Evergreen
Fresh Foliage	Fuchsia	Golden Brown	Green	Green Forest & Pine Green	Hauser Green Medium
Lemon & Lemon Custard	Licorice (Black)	Lilac Love	Linen	Magenta	Maple Syrup
Maroon	Metallic Inca Gold	Patina	Pepper Red	Plum Vineyard	Orange & Pure Orange
Purple Lilac	Red	Red-Purple	Saffron Yellow	School Bus Yellow	Tangerine
Thicket	Turquoise	Yellow	Yellow Ochre	Violet Pansy	Wicker White

Brushes

Use the best quality brushes you can buy, and take care of them. All types of glass paints used in this book can be cleaned up with soap and water, so it is easy to keep your brushes in good condition.

Glass paints tend to "lift" so it is best to use as few strokes as possible. Use the largest size brush that feels comfortable; your goal is to fill the design area with paint in a single stroke rather than many small strokes.

Brushes come in a variety of types and sizes. The basic brushes used for the projects in this book include:

Photos of brushes are in the same order as described below. They are shown slightly smaller than actual size.

Round: Sizes 2, 4, 6, 8, 10
Round brushes have a round ferrule with hairs that come to a point. They are excellent for basecoating, painting details, and small areas such as the tips of leaves and hearts.

Script Liner: Sizes 2/0, 0
The script liner is a long-haired round brush used for detail work such as scrolls, spirals, and swirls. It is used with paint thinned to an ink-like consistency with a thinning medium. To load the brush, roll the script liner into the thinned paint, pulling toward you. Hold the brush perpendicular to your painting surface and apply light pressure to paint the design.

Liner: Sizes 2, 4, 6
A liner brush has slightly shorter hairs than a script liner. The hairs come to a fine point and the brush creates delicate, slender lines that are excellent for line work, lettering, outlining, adding details and flowing lines for eyes, vines, etc. To load the brush, roll the hairs into paint thinned with a thinning medium, pulling toward you. Hold the brush perpendicular to your painting surface and apply light pressure to paint the design.

Angular: Sizes ⅛", ¼", ½", ¾"
An angular brush is a flat brush that is cut at an angle. This brush is used to float or side-load. Dip the brush into the medium formulated for the paint you are using. Blend back and forth on the palette. Tip the longest edge of the brush into the paint, then blend back and forth, working the paint into the bristles. The paint should remain predominantly on one side of the brush, gradually blending to the other side. Angled brushes can also be used to walk out a float. (See *Definitions and Techniques.*)

Flat (Bright): Sizes 4, 6, 10
Flats are rectangular shaped brushes that have a chisel edge. They are used for basecoating, wide stripes, and stroke leaves.

Square Wash: Size 1"
A wash brush is used for basecoating large areas or applying sealers. Dip the brush in the medium formulated for the paint you are using, and blot the excess on a paper towel. Dip the brush into the paint, blend into the bristles, and paint the desired areas on your design.

Other Painting Tools

You can use tools other than brushes to apply paint when you want to create a special effect, a uniform or repeated shape, or a texture.

Tip Pen Set

Tip pen sets are self-threading metal tips that can be used with a variety of types of paint to let you write and make fine detailed lines with paint. You can also purchase reusable bottles that attach to these tips to hold your paint. To use the tip pen, remove the cap from the plastic paint bottle and attach the metal tip in its place. Squeeze the paint bottle gently as you draw with the metal tip.

Dauber

This paint applicator looks like a dowel with a small rounded sponge on one end. Daubers generally come in ¼" and ½" sizes. To use the dauber, dip the sponge in the paint color of your choice, off-load on your palette to remove excess paint, and dab on a nice rounded dot of color.

Sponge Applicator

The sponge applicator is a round sponge on a dowel. The painting surface of the sponge is flat rather than domed. Sponge applicators come in various sizes. To use the tool, dab the flat surface of the sponge into the paint, offload it on your palette to remove excess paint, then dab to form a uniform round dot on your surface.

Masking Tape

Masking tape is used to mask off certain areas. In the decorative painting section of craft shops, there is a variety of sizes available, beginning at ⅛" wide. The various widths are great for making stripes and plaids.

Pictured above, clockwise from top left: Sponge applicator, ⅛" masking tape, daubers.

Sea Sponge

Apply paint with a natural sea sponge for a softly textured effect. Moisten the sponge with water to soften it, then squeeze out the water so the sponge is barely damp. Dab it into the paint, offload on the palette to remove excess paint, and apply to the surface in overlapping dabbing motions.

Miscellaneous Basic Supplies

For Preparing Surfaces

You'll need **paper towels** and **rubbing alcohol** to wipe surfaces before you transfer the designs and begin to paint.

For Transferring Designs

Use **tracing paper** and a **fine point black permanent pen** or a **pencil** to trace patterns from the book.

Transfer paper is a thin paper, coated on one side with chalk or graphite that is used for transferring designs. It comes in a variety of brands, colors, and sizes and can be purchased in large sheets, rolls, and smaller packages that have an assortment of colors.

I prefer the type of transfer paper that makes lines that can be removed with water. The other type leaves wax-free lines that can be removed with a **kneaded eraser.** Both kinds work well, as the lines do not resist the paint.

A **stylus** is a tool with a small rounded tip that is used to transfer designs using transfer paper. I use a **red ballpoint pen** to transfer patterns; it's easy to see which pattern lines I have transferred.

Use ⅜" **painters/artists masking tape** to secure tracing paper or transfer paper to the surface, and to mask areas of the surface that are not to be painted.

For Painting

Palette paper, a **sta-wet palette**, or **Styrofoam plates** can be used as a palette for holding and mixing paints. Palette paper comes in a pad. One side of the paper is water repellent and does not allow the paint to penetrate the paper.

You'll need a **water basin** for rinsing brushes, and **paper towels** for blotting the brushes.

Use **cotton swabs** to get into small areas to clean up paint or mistakes.

Surfaces

Clear glass and glazed ceramic items are readily available, inexpensive, and come in a wide variety of sizes and shapes. Look for new pieces in craft stores, department stores, and outlet stores. You can also buy items to paint at garage sales or rummage sales. You may need to give them a little extra cleaning before you get out your paint brushes.

Glass

Glass items include vases, jars, plates, pitchers, decanters and glasses, among many other useful and attractive forms. They may be plain or embossed with designs or borders. Glass may be clear or opaque, and comes in many colors. Much of the colored glassware has the color mixed with the glass itself; other pieces have the color painted on. When you are choosing an item to paint, avoid the painted glassware. Cleaning the surface with rubbing alcohol may remove the paint, and these commercially painted items should not be baked in your home oven.

Glazed Ceramics

You can find mugs, bowls, vases, and decorative boxes in a variety of colors at craft stores and department stores. These, too, can be plain or have decorative or embossed borders and design elements.

Tiles

Painted ceramic tiles make handsome gifts for the home. They can be used as wall decorations or cold trivets. Look for ceramic tiles at home improvement stores.

Preparing the Surface for Painting

Wipe clean glass or glazed ceramic surfaces with rubbing alcohol on a paper towel. It removes any greasy residue or traces of oil from your fingers that can keep the paint from adhering properly to the surface. After you have wiped it with alcohol, try to avoid touching the areas of the surface that you will be painting.

If you are using an item that has an extreme amount of dirt or grime-for example, something that came from a flea market or a thrift store-wash it first with dish detergent and warm water. Let it dry before you wipe it with rubbing alcohol.

Using the Patterns

This book includes patterns for all the projects. Use a photocopy machine to enlarge or reduce the pattern if necessary to fit your project.

Trace the pattern from the book onto tracing paper with a black fine point permanent pen so the pattern lines won't smear when you are transferring them. The surfaces of glass or ceramic items are often curved, so it is helpful to cut excess tracing paper away from the design.

Option 1: Transferring the Pattern

Use a transfer paper that leaves wax-free, greaseless lines that are easy to remove or erase. Use dark transfer paper for clear or light-colored surfaces, and white or light-colored transfer paper for dark-colored surfaces.

Position the traced pattern on the surface and secure it in place with tape at the top edge. Place the transfer paper between the tracing and the surface, shiny side down. Retrace the pattern with a stylus or a ballpoint pen to transfer it to the surface.

Option 2: Placing the Pattern Behind Glass

Place the traced pattern behind a clear glass surface, with the right side of the design facing to the front (inside a glass jar, for example). Tape the pattern in place. You will be able to see the pattern through the glass and follow it as you paint.

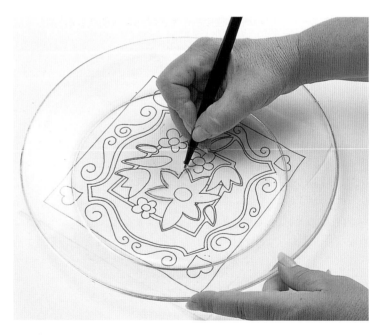

Option 3: Freehand Drawing

For a very simple design, use the pattern as a reference as you draw the design directly onto the surface with a fine point marker (not permanent). If you feel confident, paint directly on the surface without the aid of pattern lines.

Definitions and Techniques

Basecoating: Applying a solid color to an area of the design.

Floating: Creating a soft gradation of color with a single brush stroke. (This technique is also known as sideloading.) Dip your brush into the paint manufacturer's recommended medium for thinning the type of paint you are using. Blend into your brush by stroking back and forth on your palette. Tip one corner of the brush to the puddle of paint. (If you are using an angular brush, tip the long corner into the paint.) Stroke your brush back and forth on a clear space on the palette, working the paint into the bristles until there is a soft gradation from color on one side of the brush to the clear medium on the other side of the brush.

Walking out a float: Bringing a float out farther into the design area as opposed to keeping the float at the edge of the design area.

Reverse Painting

When all the color is on the back of the plate, food never touches the paint. The reverse painting technique used for the clear glass plate projects in this book is quite simple. Because the plate is clear glass, you don't need to transfer the design.

HERE'S HOW

1. Trace the pattern onto tracing paper.
2. Tape the design right side up to the front of the plate.
3. Turn the plate over - you can see through the plate and the tracing paper to follow the design as you paint on the *back* of the plate. If there is any lettering on your pattern, it should read backwards from the back side of the plate.

Happy Mother's Day Plate. See Page 66 for complete project instructions.

Step 1: Use the tip pen to outline the design elements and the lettering on the back side of the plate. The lettering is reversed. *(Back view)*

Step 2: Float the colors inside the outlines on the back side of the plate. *(Back view)*

Sponging

Using sponges to stamp on a design is a quick way to add texture and design to the surface. Compressed sponges are easy to use and can be cut into any shape. Simply cut them, place in water to decompress, load with paint, and sponge. If you merely want overall texture, and not a shape, use a sea sponge to sponge on color and texture. Here a sponge was used to stamp textured squares to the surface of a clear glass vase.

HERE'S HOW

1. Draw or transfer a shape to a compressed sponge. Use scissors to cut design, or if cutting a straight edge, use a metal ruler and a craft knife to cut out shape. Dip the sponge shape in water to decompress. Squeeze out excess moisture.

Notice how the sponge has decompressed.

2. Place a puddle of paint onto palette. Dip the sponge shape into the paint puddle to load it. Dab the sponge on a clean place on the palette to distribute paint evenly and remove excess paint.

This Owl and the Moon Candle Holder is perfect for your Halloween table. See detailed instructions for the project on page 86.

3. Press the sponge onto your surface to add a shape of color and texture.

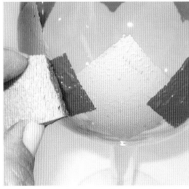

4. If you wish to add overlapping shapes, allow the first shapes to dry slightly before stamping on top of them. Acrylic enamel paint is rich and thick so that it usually covers in one coat.

Stenciling

Stenciling is an easy way to apply a design to a surface. For the best results on glass, use a simple one-overlay stencil and pounce the paint onto the glass with a sponge applicator.

SUPPLIES

Acrylic Enamel Colors:
Azure Blue
Calypso Sky
Coffee Bean

Surfaces:
Set of 4 white ceramic canisters,
    4¾" x 5¼", 4¾" x 6", 4¾" x 7",
    4¾" x 8"
Clear glass cheese shaker, 3½" tall x
    2½" diameter
Clear glass salt & pepper shakers,
    4½" tall x 1½" diameter

Brushes:
Round - #2

Other Supplies:
Rubbing alcohol
Tracing paper
Transfer paper
Clear contact paper
Decoupage scissors (or craft knife
    and cutting mat)
Sponge applicator

The paisley designs on these stencils have been cut from contact paper to make this "Purely Paisley" canister set. The details on the canisters such as the dots and comma strokes were done with a round brush.

HERE'S HOW TO CUT THE STENCIL

1. Trace the pattern and transfer the design to the contact paper.
2. Cut out the curved teardrop shapes with scissors or a craft knife.
3. Discard the teardrop shape. You will use the contact paper with the teardrop-shaped hole as your stencil. For easy placement on the surface, use an individual stencil for each teardrop. Use the smaller patterns on the smaller surfaces.

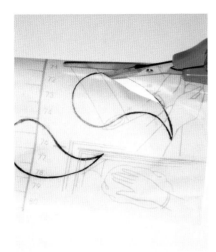

Step 1: Following the transferred pattern lines, cut out the stencil. Discard the teardrop shape.

Step 2: Peel the backing from the contact paper. Press the stencils randomly over the surface. Be sure you have good adhesion to the glass.

Step 3: Pounce on the paint with the sponge applicator.

Pattern for Paisley Canister Set

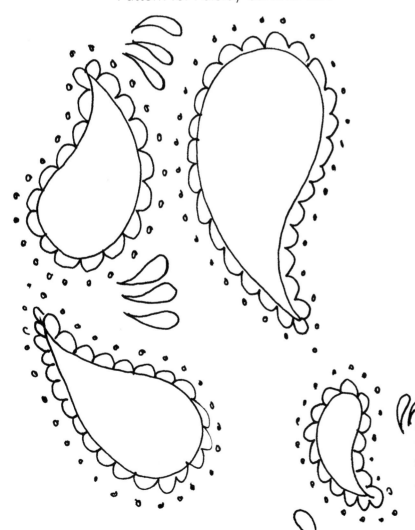

PAISLEY SET INSTRUCTIONS

1. Clean the surfaces with rubbing alcohol.
2. Adhere the stencils to the surface. Use the two largest sizes for the canisters, placed randomly. Use the small size for the salt and pepper shaker.
3. Use the sponge applicator to pounce in the teardrop shapes with Calypso Sky.
4. Dab the sponge applicator into Azure Blue and tap on the edge of each teardrop shape, blending into the Calypso Sky.
5. Remove the contact paper.
6. Use the #2 round brush and Coffee Bean to paint the linework, dots, and comma strokes around the large teardrops. Let dry.
7. Follow the manufacturer's instructions for baking or drying. ❑

Stamping

Using a Foam Stamp

A foam stamp was used to add the design to a mirror and a tile trivet. The fern is embellished with stamped ferns and brush-painted flowers. You will find foam stamps in many designs at craft stores. I used a fern stamp but any leaf or floral design would work; simply choose one in a size that fits your surface.

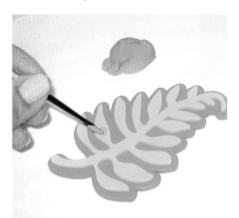

Load the stamp with paint, using a brush or cosmetic sponge. Stamp once or twice on the palette to remove excess paint.

Press the stamp onto the surface. To avoid smearing the image, lift the stamp straight up.

SUPPLIES

Acrylic Enamel Colors:
Fresh Foliage
Hauser Green Medium
Lemon Custard
Purple Lilac
Wicker White

HERE'S HOW

1. Clean the surface with rubbing alcohol.
2. Stamp the fern pattern with Fresh Foliage. Let dry.
3. Using a #2 round brush, paint a small line of Hauser Green Medium under the bottom edge of each tiny fern leaf.
4. Load the #2 round brush with Purple Lilac. Using the tip of the brush, paint each flower petal with an individual stroke, beginning at the outer tip of the petal and pulling the brush toward the flower center.
5. Dot the centers of the flowers with Lemon Custard.
6. Paint the tiny dots around the flowers with Wicker White.
7. Follow the manufacturer's instructions for baking or drying. ❑

"Dream"
Ceramic Mug

SUPPLIES

Acrylic Enamel Colors:
Azure Blue
Baby Pink
Calypso Sky
Licorice
Magenta
Purple Lilac

School Bus Yellow
Violet Pansy
Yellow Ochre

Surface:
Glazed ceramic mug

Brushes:
Round - #2
Angular - ¼"

Other Supplies:
Rubbing alcohol
Tracing paper
Transfer paper
Flow medium
Clear medium
Tip Pen set

Paint this cheerful mug for your busiest friend, as a reminder to take a break. It's great for coffee, tea, or cocoa-or you could fill it with colored pencils and glitter pens to inspire daydreaming doodles.

PREPARATION

1. Clean the surface with rubbing alcohol.
2. Trace the pattern and transfer the design.

PAINT THE DESIGN

Star, Dots & Stripes:

1. Basecoat the large star, two of the stripes on the handle, and some of the dots with Calypso Sky.
2. Float the bottom of the star, the top edges of the stripes, and the bottom edges of the dots with Azure Blue.

Heart, Dots & Stripes:

1. Basecoat the heart, two of the stripes on the handle, and some of the dots with Baby Pink.
2. Float the bottom edges of the heart and dots with Magenta.
3. Float the top edges of the pink stripes on the handle with Magenta.

Moon, Dots & Stripe:

1. Basecoat the moon, one stripe on the handle, and some of the dots with School Bus Yellow.
2. Float the bottom edge of the moon and dots with Yellow Ochre.
3. Float the top edge of the stripe with Yellow Ochre.

Swirl, Dots & Stripes:

1. Basecoat the swirl, two stripes on the handle, and some of the dots with Purple Lilac.
2. Float the bottom edge of the swirl and dots with Violet Pansy.
3. Float the top edges of the stripes with Violet Pansy.

Outlines & Lettering:

1. Using the tip pen and Licorice, outline the stripes on the handle.
2. Outline and add details to the heart, star, moon, and swirl.
3. Outline the letters for the word "Dream."
4. Draw spirals on the colored dots and add small Licorice dots.

FINISH

Follow the manufacturer's instructions for baking or drying. ❑

Pattern for Dream Ceramic Mug

Bloom
Ceramic Mug

SUPPLIES

Acrylic Enamel Colors:
Baby Pink
Berry Wine
Engine Red
Fresh Foliage
Green Forest
Licorice
Magenta
School Bus Yellow
Yellow Ochre

Surface:
Glazed ceramic mug

Brushes:
Round - #2, #4
Angular - ¼"
Flat - #4

Other Supplies:
Rubbing alcohol
Tracing paper
Transfer paper
Flow medium
Clear medium
Tip Pen set

The sunny garden flowers on this handy mug-and their inspiring message-are always in season.

PREPARATION

1. Clean the surface with rubbing alcohol.
2. Trace the pattern and transfer the design.

PAINT THE DESIGN

See the Bloom Painting Worksheet.

Flowers:

1. Basecoat the tulip with Engine Red.
2. Float the bottom edge of the tulip with Berry Wine.
3. Basecoat the roses with Baby Pink.
4. While the Baby Pink paint is still wet (add another coat of Baby Pink if the first coat is dry), and using the chisel edge of your brush, blend in some Magenta.
5. Paint the daisy petals with School Bus Yellow.
6. Float the bases of the daisy petals closest to the center with Yellow Ochre.

Leaves:

1. Basecoat the leaves with Fresh Foliage.
2. Float the bases of the leaves closest to the flowers with Green Forest.

Handle:

1. Basecoat two stripes with Engine Red.

2. Float one side of each Engine Red stripe with Berry Wine.
3. Basecoat two of the stripes with Baby Pink.
4. Float one side of each Baby Pink stripe with Magenta.
5. Paint two stripes with School Bus Yellow.
6. Float one side of each School Bus Yellow stripe with Yellow Ochre.

Outlines & Lettering:

1. Using the tip pen and Licorice, outline the stripes on the handle.
2. Outline and add details to the leaves and the flowers.
3. Outline the letters for the word "Bloom."
4. Add the small dots and swirls.

FINISH

Follow the manufacturer's instructions for baking or drying. ❏

Pattern for Bloom Ceramic Mug

BLOOM PAINTING WORKSHEET

Basecoat the tulip with Engine Red.

Basecoat the leaves with Fresh Foliage.

Basecoat the rose with Baby Pink.

While the paint is wet, blend Magenta into the Baby Pink with the chisel edge of the brush.

Float the bases of the petals with Yellow Ochre.

Float inside of leaves with Green Forest.

Basecoat the petals with School Bus Yellow.

Float the bottom edge of the tulip with Berry Wine.

Using the tip pen with Licorice, outline the flowers and paint the lettering and details.

PARTY HAT PAINTING WORKSHEET

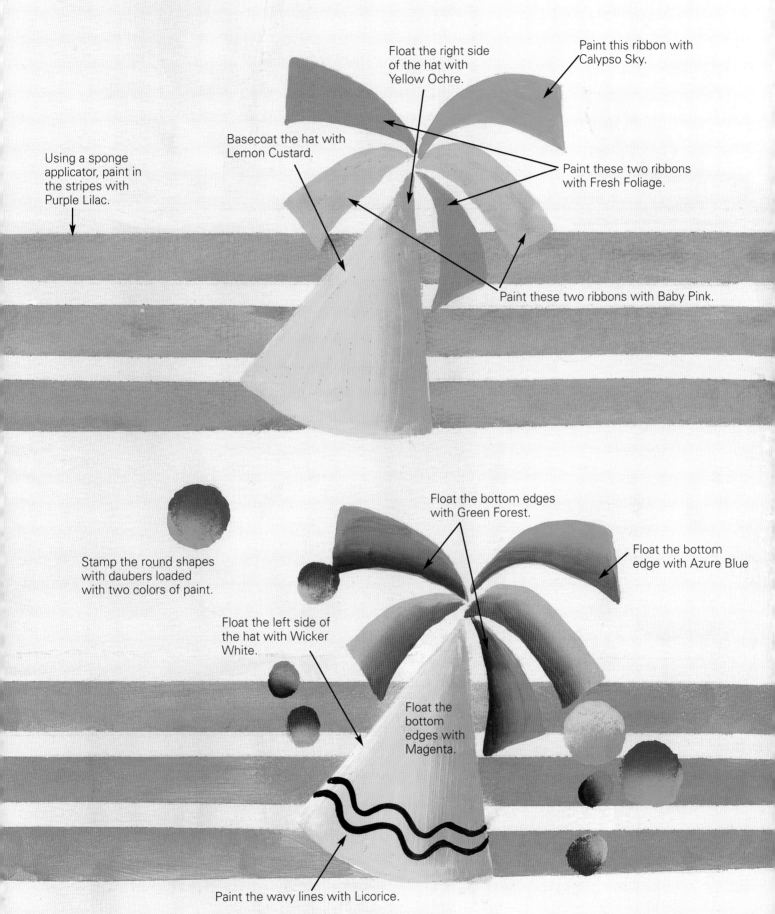

Float the right side of the hat with Yellow Ochre.

Paint this ribbon with Calypso Sky.

Basecoat the hat with Lemon Custard.

Paint these two ribbons with Fresh Foliage.

Using a sponge applicator, paint in the stripes with Purple Lilac.

Paint these two ribbons with Baby Pink.

Float the bottom edges with Green Forest.

Float the bottom edge with Azure Blue

Stamp the round shapes with daubers loaded with two colors of paint.

Float the left side of the hat with Wicker White.

Float the bottom edges with Magenta.

Paint the wavy lines with Licorice.

Make a Wish

Cake Stand & Candy Jar

SUPPLIES

Acrylic Enamel Colors:

Azure Blue

Baby Pink

Calypso Sky

Fresh Foliage

Green Forest

Lemon Custard

Licorice

Magenta

Purple Lilac

Wicker White

Yellow Ochre

Surfaces:

Clear glass cake stand with
  lid, 12" tall x 9" diameter

Wide mouth mason jar with
  lid
  (no decoration or pattern
  on the glass)

Brushes:

Round - #2, #4

Angular - ¼"

Liner - #2

Other Supplies:

Rubbing alcohol

Tracing paper

Sponge applicator

Daubers, variety of sizes

Masking tape or grout tape,
  ¼"

Ribbon

This cake stand and candy jar make any birthday a special occasion!
Bake a wonderful cake, then deliver it in the perfect cake stand with a
jar of delicious candies to complement it.

PREPARATION

1. Clean the glass surfaces with rubbing alcohol.
2. Trace the pattern.
3. Tape the tracing to the inside of the cake lid and candy jar with the right side
   of the design facing outward.
4. Using the pattern as a guide, place three pieces of tape around the lid of the
   cake stand horizontally.
5. Using a sponge applicator, pounce a thin coat of Purple Lilac between the
   taped lines. Remove the tape.

PAINT THE DESIGN

Hat:
See the Party Hat Painting Worksheet.
  1. Basecoat the hat with Lemon Custard.
  2. Float the right side of the hat with Yellow Ochre.
  3. Float the left side of the hat with Wicker White.
  4. Paint the wavy lines on the hat with Licorice.
  5. Paint two of the ribbons coming from the top of the hat with Fresh Foliage.
  6. Float one side of each Fresh Foliage ribbon with Green Forest.
  7. Paint two of the ribbons with Baby Pink.
  8. Float one side of each Baby Pink ribbon with Magenta.
  9. Paint one of the ribbons with Calypso Sky.
  10. Float one side of the Calypso Sky ribbon with Azure Blue.

Lettering & Dots:
  1. Paint the lettering with Licorice. Let dry.
  2. Using two sizes of daubers, paint the dots around the lid of the cake stand.
     Dip one half of the dauber in one color and the other half into another color,
     off-load onto your palette to remove excess paint and blend the colors, then
     stamp the dots randomly around the stripes. Use these color combinations:
     Baby Pink/Magenta, Calypso Sky/Azure Blue, Fresh Foliage/Green Forest, and
     Yellow Ochre/Lemon Custard.

FINISH

1. Paint the knob on the cake lid with Purple Lilac.
2. Follow the manufacturer's instructions for baking or drying.
3. Tie ribbon around the cake lid knob and around the candy jar lid. ❑

Pattern for Make a Wish Cake Stand & Candy Jar

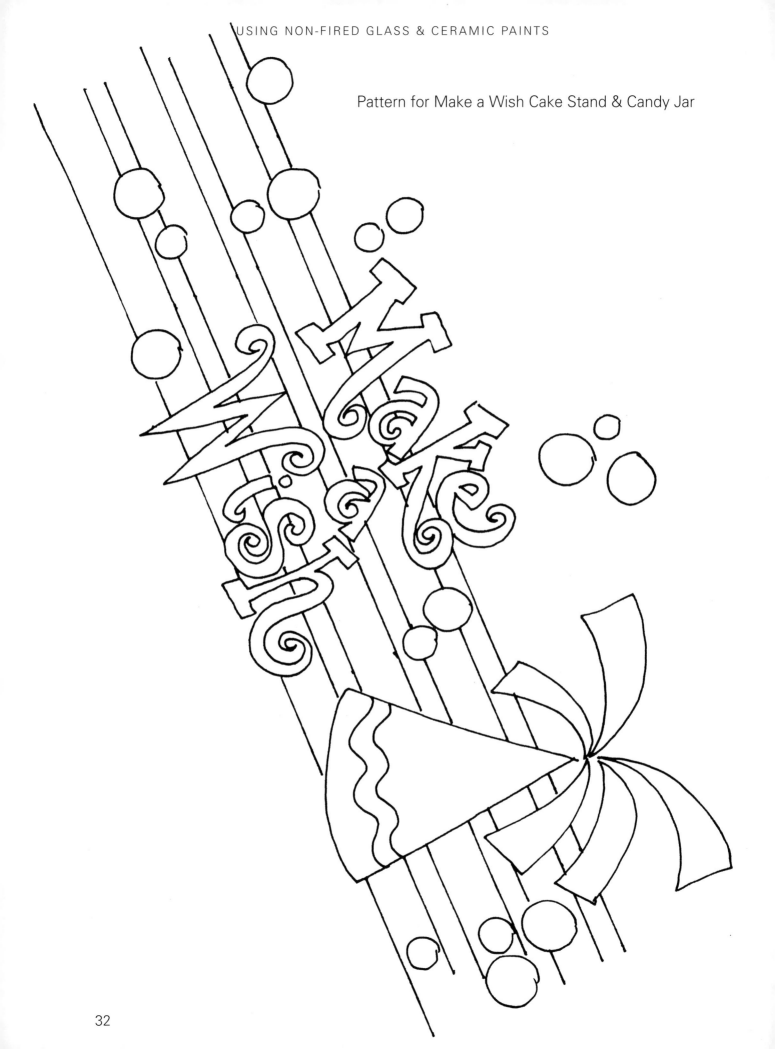

Pattern for Love Love Plate
Enlarge at 133% for actual size

Love Love

Plate

SUPPLIES

Acrylic Enamel Colors:
Baby Pink
Licorice
Magenta
Wicker White

Surface:
Clear glass plate, 10"

Brushes:
Angular - ¼"
Round - #2

Other Supplies:
Rubbing alcohol
Tracing paper
Painters tape
Flow medium
Clear medium

Serve up a sweet treat for your valentine on a "love-ly" plate. This reverse painting technique is as simple as coloring inside the lines.

PREPARATION

1. Clean the glass surface with rubbing alcohol.
2. Trace the pattern.
3. Tape the tracing to the front of the plate. Turn the plate over. You will be able to see the design through the tracing paper from the back of the plate. Note that the lettering will read backwards from the back side of the plate.

PAINT THE DESIGN

Paint on the back side of the plate.
1. Outline the hearts, designs and lettering, using the tip pen with Licorice. Let dry.
2. Staying within the black outline, float one side of each heart with Wicker White.
3. Float the other side of each heart with Magenta. Let dry.
4. Paint over the entire heart with Baby Pink. Let dry.

FINISH

Follow the manufacturer's instructions for baking or drying. Turn the plate over and enjoy the design. ❏

Pattern for Bunny in the Garden Container

Bunny in the Garden
Container

SUPPLIES

Acrylic Enamel Colors:
Baby Pink
Berry Wine
Hauser Green Medium
Lemon Custard
Licorice
Lilac Love
Linen
Maple Syrup
Purple Lilac
Thicket
Violet Pansy
Wicker White

Surface:
Glazed ceramic vase, 9" x 9"

Brushes:
Angular - ⅛", ¼"
Round - #4
Liner - #2
Script liner - 2/0

Other Supplies:
Clear Medium
Flow Medium
Tracing Paper
Blue Transfer Paper
Rubbing Alcohol

PREPARATION

1. Clean ceramic surface with rubbing alcohol.
2. Trace the design on to tracing paper. Trace over the design to transfer design to ceramic surface using the blue transfer paper.

PAINT THE DESIGN

Rabbit:
1. Basecoat the rabbit Linen using a #4 round brush.
2. Float the outer edges of the rabbit body using a ¼" angular brush with Maple Syrup.
3. Basecoat the inside of the ears and nose Baby Pink using a #2 round. Float the outer edges of the inside of the ears using a ⅛" angular brush with a 50/50 mix of Maple Syrup and Berry Wine. Float the bottom edge of the nose using a ⅛" angular brush with the same mix. Using Wicker White and ⅛" angular brush, float around the center line for the mouth, just under the nose. Add Flow Medium if necessary to thin the paint when floating.
4. Paint the eyes Wicker White using a #2/0 round. Paint the inside of the eyes Maple Syrup using a #2/0 script liner. Paint the iris of the eyes Licorice with the 2/0 script liner. Paint a highlight in the iris Wicker White using a #2/0 script liner.
5. Paint the whiskers, mouth, and eyelashes Maple Syrup using a #2 liner.

Flowers:
1. Basecoat the flowers with the #4 round brush using Lilac Love.
2. Float the inside of the petals (closest to the center) using a ¼" angular brush and Violet Pansy. Use Flow Medium to thin the paint if necessary when floating.
3. Float the outer edges of the petals (tips) with Purple Lilac using the ¼" angular brush.
4. Paint a Wicker White highlight at the tips of the petals using a 2/0 script liner brush.
5. Using a 2/0 script liner, paint the lines in the petals coming from the center of the flower Violet Pansy.
6. Paint the stamen in the flower Maple Syrup using a 2/0 liner brush. Paint a highlight on the stamen and the dots at the end of the stamen with a 2/0 liner using Lemon Custard.

Leaves:
1. Basecoat the leaves Hauser Green Medium using a #4 round brush.
2. Float one side of the leaves with a 50/50 mix of Thicket and Maple Syrup using a ¼" angular brush.
3. Float the other side of the leaves Lemon Custard using the ¼" angular brush.
4. Paint the line in the center of the leaves using a #2 liner and Lemon Custard.

FINISH

1. To acquire a glossy finish that will help to seal the design, paint one coat of Clear Medium over the entire design.
2. Follow manufacturer's instructions on paint bottle for baking and drying paints. ❑

Kiss a Frog
Candy Jar

SUPPLIES

Acrylic Enamel Colors:

Azure Blue

Baby Pink

Fresh Foliage

Green Forest

Lemon Custard

Licorice

Lilac Love

Magenta

Patina

Pure Orange

Wicker White

Yellow Ochre

Surface:

Large clear glass jar with lid, 11" tall (with lid) x 8" diameter

Brushes:

Round - #2, # 6

Angular - ⅛", ¼", ½"

Liner - # 2

Other Supplies:

Rubbing alcohol

Tracing paper

Painters tape

Give this kissable frog on a candy jar to a friend who has a great sense of humor. Be sure to fill it with their favorite treats. If you have a health conscious friend, fill it with your favorite home made granola.

PREPARATION

1. Clean the glass surfaces with rubbing alcohol.
2. Trace the patterns.
3. Tape the tracings to the inside of the jar and lid with the right side of the design facing outward.

PAINT THE DESIGN

Frog:
See the Frog Painting Worksheet.
1. Basecoat the frog body with Fresh Foliage.
2. Float Green Forest to shade the face, eyelids, body, legs, and feet.
3. Basecoat the dots on the body with Lemon Custard.
4. Float the bottom of the dots with Fresh Foliage.
5. Float the top of the frog's head, the edges of the arms, and the top of the eyelids with Lemon Custard.
6. Basecoat the lips and cheeks with Baby Pink.
7. Float the top of the lips and cheeks with Wicker White.
8. Float the bottom of the lips and cheeks with Magenta.
9. Paint the line in the mouth (for the grin) with Magenta.

Frog Eyes:
See the Frog Painting Worksheet.
1. Basecoat the irises with Patina.
2. Float the top of the irises (near the eyelid) with Azure Blue.
3. Basecoat the whites of the eyes with Wicker White.
4. Basecoat the pupils with Licorice.
5. Paint a white highlight in each pupil with Wicker White.
6. Outline the irises, paint the lines in the irises and the eyelashes with Licorice.

Stars, Stripes, Swirls & Dots:
1. Basecoat the stars with Lemon Custard.
2. Float the bottom edges of the stars with Yellow Ochre.
3. Paint the swirls on the lid and some of the swirls on the jar with Pure Orange.
4. Paint the stripes on the lid and the some of the swirls on the jar with Lilac Love.
5. Float one side of the stripes with Violet Pansy.
6. Paint the dots around the knob on the lid with Lemon Custard.

FINISH

Follow the manufacturer's instructions for baking or drying. ❏

FROG PAINTING WORKSHEET

Basecoat the frog with Fresh Foliage.

Basecoat the irises with Patina. Float the tops of the irises with Azure Blue.

Paint the pupils, outline the irises, and add lines to the irises with Licorice.

Paint Wicker White highlights in the pupils.

Basecoat the dots on the frog and the star with Lemon Custard.

Basecoat the cheeks and lips with Baby Pink. Float the top edges with Wicker White.

Float the bottoms of the cheeks with Magenta.

Float the bottom edges of the spots with Fresh Foliage.

Float shading with Green Forest.

Paint the eyelashes with Licorice.

Paint the line in the mouth with Magenta.

Float Green Forest on the outside of the legs and the bottoms of the feet

Float the bottom of the star with Yellow Ochre.

Float the tops of the feet with Lemon Custard.

40

Pattern for Kiss a Frog Candy Jar
Enlarge at 133% for actual size

Lid Pattern
Enlarge at 133%
for actual size

Fruit of the Vine
Wine Glasses & Carafe

SUPPLIES

Acrylic Enamel Colors:

Fresh Foliage

Linen

Maple Syrup

Metallic Inca Gold

Plum Vineyard

Purple Lilac

Thicket

Violet Pansy

Wicker White

Surfaces:

Clear wine glasses, 9" tall x 3¼"
    diameter

Clear wine carafe, 11" tall x 7" wide

Brushes:

Round - #2, #5

Angular - ¼"

Liner - 2/0

Other Supplies:

Rubbing alcohol

Tracing paper

Blue painters tape

Tip Pen set

Flow medium

Clear medium

Follow the steps on the painting worksheet to create round, juicy grapes on gifts for the wine-lovers on your list. Use a photocopier to enlarge or reduce the pattern to fit any size carafe and glasses.

PREPARATION

1. Clean the glass surfaces with rubbing alcohol.
2. Trace the pattern.
3. Tape the tracing to the inside of the glass with the right side of the design facing outward.

PAINT THE DESIGN

Grapes & Stem:

See the Grapes Painting Worksheet.

1. Basecoat the grapes with Purple Lilac.
2. Float the bottom edges of the grapes with Plum Vineyard, walking the float about two-thirds up on the grape. Let dry.
3. Float the bottom edges of the grapes again with Violet Pansy, floating only about one-third of the way up on the grape.
4. Mix 2 parts Wicker White + 1 part Purple Lilac. Add the highlights to the tops of the grapes.
5. Basecoat the stem with Linen.
6. Float the bottom edge of the stem with Maple Syrup.

Leaves & Tendrils:

See the Grapes Painting Worksheet.

1. Basecoat the leaves with Fresh Foliage.
2. Float the outer edges of the leaves with Thicket.
3. Paint the leaf veins with Thicket.
4. Mix Wicker White 50/50 with Thicket. Paint the highlights in the centers of the leaf veins.
5. Using the tip pen and Metallic Inca Gold, paint the curly tendrils and tiny dots around the grapes.

FINISH

Follow the manufacturer's instructions for baking or drying. ❑

GRAPES PAINTING WORKSHEET

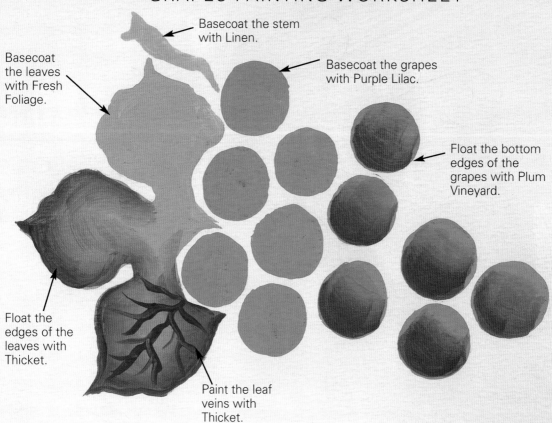

Basecoat the stem with Linen.

Basecoat the leaves with Fresh Foliage.

Basecoat the grapes with Purple Lilac.

Float the bottom edges of the grapes with Plum Vineyard.

Float the edges of the leaves with Thicket.

Paint the leaf veins with Thicket.

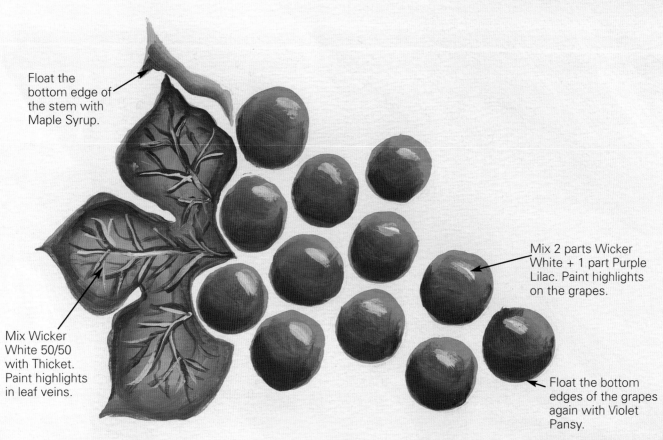

Float the bottom edge of the stem with Maple Syrup.

Mix 2 parts Wicker White + 1 part Purple Lilac. Paint highlights on the grapes.

Mix Wicker White 50/50 with Thicket. Paint highlights in leaf veins.

Float the bottom edges of the grapes again with Violet Pansy.

Pattern for Fruit of the Vine Carafe
Enlarge pattern 133% for actual size

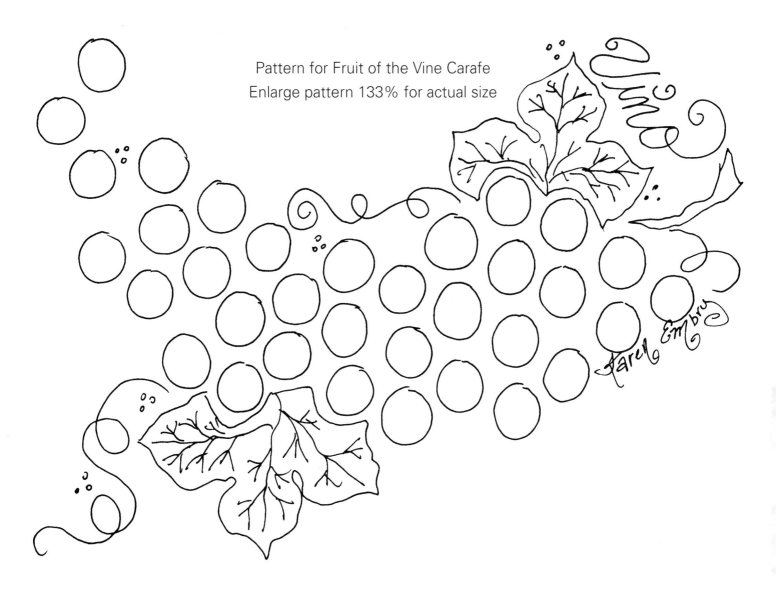

Pattern for Fruit of the Vine Wine Glass
Enlarge pattern 133% for actual size

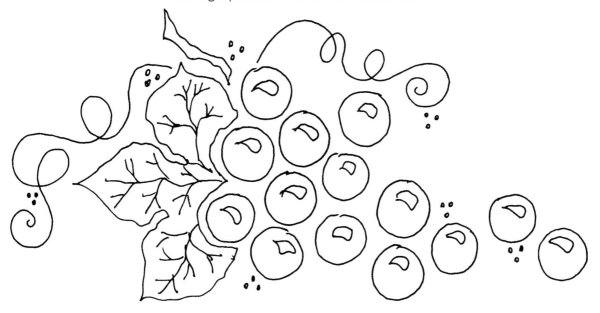

Citrus Delight
Pitcher & Glasses

SUPPLIES

Acrylic Enamel Colors:
Butter Pecan
Coffee Bean
Fresh Foliage
Green Forest
Lemon Custard
Pure Orange
Tangerine
Yellow Ochre

Surfaces:
Clear glass pitcher
Clear glass mugs,
    5" tall x 4" diameter

Brushes:
Round - #2, #4
Angular - ⅛", ¼", ½"
Script liner - #2/0

Other Supplies:
Rubbing alcohol
Tracing paper
Blue painters tape
Flow medium
Clear medium

This clear glass set makes me think of long summer afternoons, and lemonade on a shady porch. Present it to the hostess whenever you are invited to an outdoor dinner gathering.

PREPARATION

1. Clean the glass surfaces with rubbing alcohol.
2. Trace the pattern.
3. Tape the tracing to the inside of the glass with the right side of the design facing outward.

PAINT THE DESIGN

Lemons:
See the Lemon Painting Worksheet.
1. Basecoat the lemons with Lemon Custard.
2. Float the bottom edges of the lemons with Yellow Ochre.

Oranges:
1. Basecoat the oranges with Tangerine.
2. Float the bottom edges of the oranges with Pure Orange, walking the float about one-third of the way up.

Vines, Leaves & Stems:
See the Lemon Painting Worksheet.
1. Basecoat the vines and leaves with Fresh Foliage.
2. Accent the bottom edges of the vines with a thin line of Green Forest.
3. Paint the center veins in the leaves with Green Forest.
4. Float the bottom edges of the leaves with Green Forest.
5. Accent the top edges of the vines with a thin line of Lemon Custard.
6. Float the top edge of the leaves and just below the leaf veins with Lemon Custard.
7. Paint the stems with Butter Pecan.
8. Float the bottom edges of the stems with Coffee Bean.

FINISH

Follow the manufacturer's instructions for baking or drying. ❏

LEMON PAINTING WORKSHEET

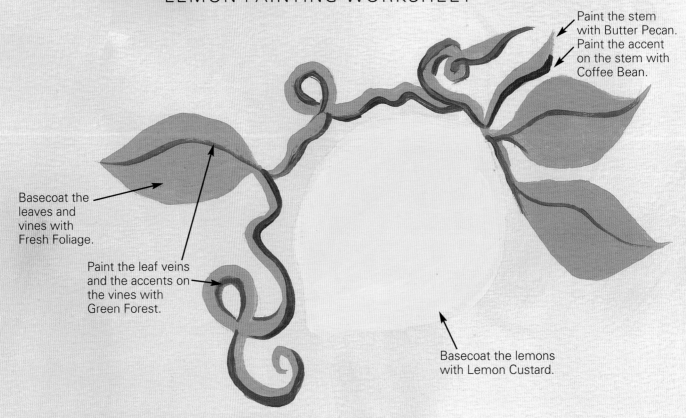

Paint the stem with Butter Pecan. Paint the accent on the stem with Coffee Bean.

Basecoat the leaves and vines with Fresh Foliage.

Paint the leaf veins and the accents on the vines with Green Forest.

Basecoat the lemons with Lemon Custard.

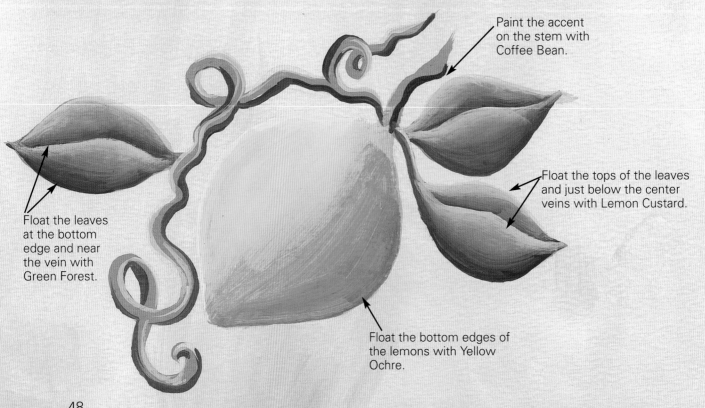

Paint the accent on the stem with Coffee Bean.

Float the tops of the leaves and just below the center veins with Lemon Custard.

Float the leaves at the bottom edge and near the vein with Green Forest.

Float the bottom edges of the lemons with Yellow Ochre.

Pattern for Citrus Delight Glasses
Enlarge pattern 133% for actual size

Pattern for Citrus Delight Pitcher
Enlarge pattern 133% for actual size

ABC
Baby's Food Jars

SUPPLIES

Acrylic Enamel Colors:

Azure Blue

Baby Pink

Berry Wine

Calypso Sky

Engine Red

Fresh Foliage

Green Forest

Lemon Custard

Licorice

Linen

Magenta

Maple Syrup

Purple Lilac

Violet Pansy

Wicker White

Yellow Ochre

Surfaces:

Clear glass storage jars with plastic
    lids

Brushes:

Round - #2

Angular - ⅛", ¼"

Liner - #2

Other Supplies:

Rubbing alcohol

Tracing paper

Blue painters tape

Flow medium

Clear medium

Happy colors transform these glass dishes from practical to playful! Paint a set of baby food storage jars with four different designs, coordinated by style and color.

PREPARATION

1. Clean the glass surfaces with rubbing alcohol.
2. Trace the pattern.
3. Tape the tracing to the inside of the glass with the right side of the design facing outward.

PAINT THE DESIGN

"A" is for Apple Jar

See the Apple Painting Worksheet.

Apple:
1. Basecoat the apple with Engine Red.
2. Float the right side of the apple with Berry Wine.
3. Float the left side of the apple with Lemon Custard.
4. Basecoat the leaf with Fresh Foliage.
5. Float the bottom edge of the leaf with Green Forest.
6. Paint the leaf veins with Green Forest.
7. Basecoat the stem with Linen.
8. Float the bottom edge of the stem with Maple Syrup.
9. Paint the swirl at the top of the stem with Maple Syrup.

The Letter "A":
1. Basecoat the letter with Purple Lilac.
2. Float the right side of the letter with Violet Pansy.
3. Float the left side of the letter with Wicker White.
4. Paint the horizontal wavy lines on the letter with Wicker White.

Stripes & Wavy Lines:
1. Basecoat the stripes with Purple Lilac.
2. Float the left side of the stripes with Violet Pansy.
3. Paint the wavy lines with Wicker White.

Continued on page 54

APPLE PAINTING WORKSHEET

Float the left side of the letter "A" with Wicker White.

Paint the stem with Linen.

Basecoat the leaf with Fresh Foliage.

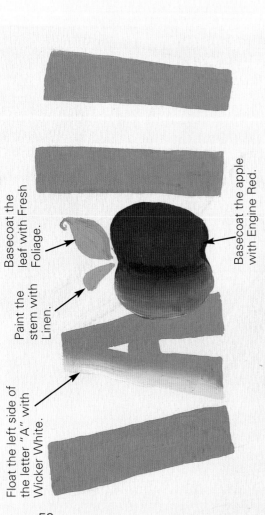

Basecoat the apple with Engine Red.

Basecoat the letter "A" and the stripes with Purple Lilac. Paint the wavy lines in the letter "A" with Wicker White.

Float the right side of the letter "A" with Violet Pansy.

Float the stem with Maple Syrup. Paint the swirl with Maple Syrup.

Float the bottom of the leaf with Green Forest. Paint the leaf veins with Green Forest.

Paint the wavy lines with Wicker White.

Float the left side of the stripes with Violet Pansy.

Float the right side of the apple with Berry Wine.

Float the left side of the apple with Lemon Custard.

BEE PAINTING WORKSHEET

Basecoat the letter "B" and the stripes with Calypso Sky.

3asecoat the bee body with Lemon Custard.

Basecoat the wings with Wicker White. Float the edges of the wings with a light gray mix of 4 parts Wicker White + 1 part Licorice.

Paint the antennae, head, stripes on body, and swirls on wings with Licorice.

Float the bottom edge of the bee body with Yellow Ochre.

Dot the eyes with Wicker White.

Paint the dots with Wicker White.

Float the left side of the letter "B" with Wicker White.

Float the right side of the letter "B" and the left side of the stripes with Azure Blue.

DUCK PAINTING WORKSHEET

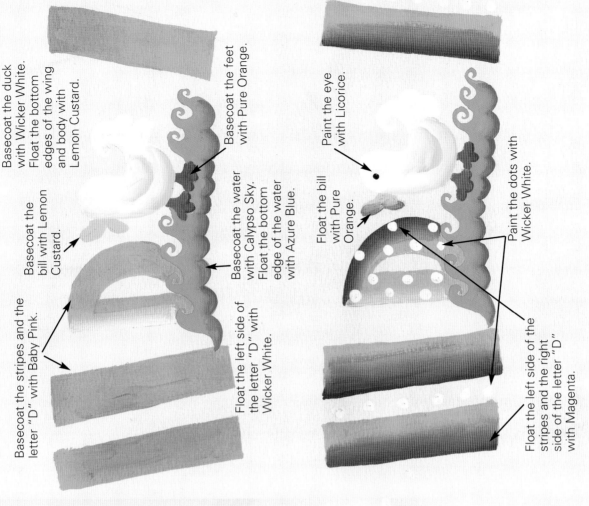

Basecoat the duck with Wicker White. Float the bottom edges of the wing and body with Lemon Custard.

Basecoat the bill with Lemon Custard.

Basecoat the feet with Pure Orange.

Basecoat the stripes and the letter "D" with Baby Pink.

Basecoat the water with Calypso Sky. Float the bottom edge of the water with Azure Blue.

Float the left side of the letter "D" with Wicker White.

Paint the eye with Licorice.

Paint the dots with Wicker White.

Float the bill with Pure Orange.

Paint the dots with Wicker White.

Float the left side of the stripes and the right side of the letter "D" with Magenta.

Float the left side of the stripes and the right side of the letter "D" with Magenta.

CAT PAINTING WORKSHEET

Float the left side of the letter "C" with Wicker White.

Float the top of the cat's head with Wicker White.

Basecoat the nose and inside the ears with Baby Pink.

Basecoat the cat with a light gray mix of 4 parts Wicker White + 1 part Licorice.

Basecoat the stripes, the letter "C", and the bow with Lemon Custard.

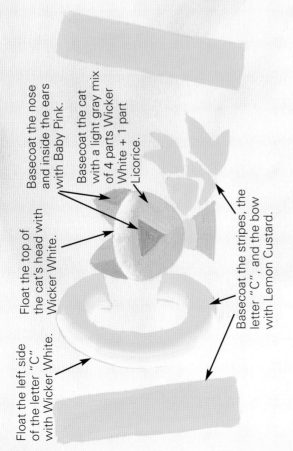

Paint the wavy lines with Wicker White.

Float the inside of the ears and the top of the nose with Magenta.

Paint the highlights in the eyes with Wicker White.

Paint the eyes and the line for the mouth with Licorice.

Float the left side of the stripes, the right side of the letter "C", and the bottom edges of the bow with Yellow Ochre.

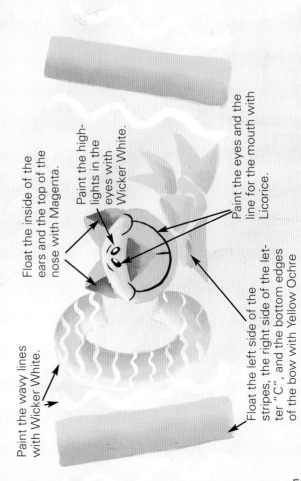

53

ABC Baby's Food Jars
Continued from page 50

"B" is for Bee Jar

See the Bee Painting Worksheet.

Bee:
1. Basecoat the bee's body with Lemon Custard.
2. Float the bottom edge of the body with Yellow Ochre.
3. Basecoat the wings with Wicker White.
4. Float the outer edges of the wings with a light gray mix of 4 parts Wicker White + 1 part Licorice.
5. Paint the bee's head, antennae, swirls around the wings, and stripes on body with Licorice.
6. Dot the eyes with Wicker White.

The Letter "B":
1. Basecoat the letter with Calypso Sky.
2. Float the right side of the letter with Azure Blue.
3. Float the left side of the letter with Wicker White.
4. Paint the dots on the letter with Wicker White.

Stripes & Dots:
1. Basecoat the stripes with Calypso Sky.
2. Float the left side of the stripes with Azure Blue.
3. Paint the dots between the stripes with Wicker White.

"C" is for Cat Jar

See the Cat Painting Worksheet.

Cat:
1. Basecoat the cat with a light gray mix of 4 parts Wicker White + 1 part Licorice.
2. Float the top of the head with Wicker White.
3. Basecoat the nose and inside the ears with Baby Pink.
4. Float the inside of the ears and the top of the nose with Magenta.
5. Paint the eyes and the lines for the mouth and eyebrows with Licorice.
6. Highlight the eyes with Wicker White.
7. Basecoat the bow with Lemon Custard.
8. Float the bottom edge of the bow with Yellow Ochre.

The Letter "C":
1. Basecoat the letter with Lemon Custard.
2. Float the right side of the letter with Yellow Ochre.
3. Float the left side of the letter with Wicker White.
4. Paint the horizontal wavy lines on the letter with Wicker White.

Stripes & Wavy Lines:
1. Basecoat the stripes with Lemon Custard.
2. Float the left side of the stripes with Yellow Ochre.
3. Paint the wavy lines between the stripes with Wicker White.

"D" is for Duck Jar

See the Duck Painting Worksheet.

Duck:
1. Basecoat the duck with Wicker White.
2. Float the bottom edge of the body and wing with Lemon Custard.
3. Basecoat the bill with Lemon Custard.
4. Float the outer part of the bill with Pure Orange.
5. Paint the feet with Pure Orange.
6. Paint the dot for the eye with Licorice.

The Letter "D":
1. Basecoat the letter with Baby Pink.
2. Float the right side of the letter with Magenta.
3. Float the left side of the letter with Wicker White.
4. Paint the dots on the letter with Wicker White.

Water:
1. Basecoat the water with Calypso Sky.
2. Float the bottom edge of the water with Azure Blue.

Stripes & Dots:
1. Basecoat the stripes with Baby Pink.
2. Float the left side of the stripes with Magenta.
3. Paint the dots between the stripes with Wicker White.

FINISH

Follow the manufacturer's instructions for baking or drying. ❏

Patterns for ABC Baby's Food Jars

Enlarge patterns 133% for actual size

Welcome Baby
Piggy Bank

SUPPLIES

Acrylic Enamel Colors:
Azure Blue
Baby Pink
Burnt Umber
Calypso Sky
Fresh Foliage
Green Forest
Lemon Custard
Licorice
Linen
Magenta
Maple Syrup
Purple Lilac
Violet Pansy
Wicker White
Yellow Ochre

Surface:
Glazed ceramic piggy bank,
    10" x 10"

Brushes:
Round - #2, #4
Angular - ⅛", ¼"
Liner - #2

Other Supplies:
Rubbing alcohol
Tracing paper
Tip Pen set
Flow medium
Clear medium
Yellow ribbon, ½" wide, ½
    yard
Thick tacky glue

Welcome your special little one with Baby's name and birth date spelled out on a puffy cloud. I have included my design for a complete alphabet, so you'll have all the letters and numbers you need to personalize this piggy.

PREPARATION

1. Clean the surface with rubbing alcohol.
2. Trace the pattern and transfer the design to both sides of the piggy bank. Do not transfer the lettering to the heart and the cloud until they have been painted and are completely dry.

PAINT THE DESIGN

Bear:
1. Basecoat the bear with Linen.
2. Float the top of the bear's head, hands, and legs with Wicker White.
3. Basecoat the nose with Maple Syrup.
4. Float the bottom edge of the nose with Burnt Umber.
5. Paint the line for the mouth with Maple Syrup.
6. Basecoat inside the ears with Baby Pink. Float the edges closest to the head with Magenta.
7. Paint the eyes, lines between fingers, and eyebrows with Burnt Umber.

Sun & Heart:
1. Basecoat the sun and heart with Lemon Custard.
2. Float the top of the sun and heart with Wicker White.
3. Float the bottom edges of the sun and heart with Yellow Ochre.
4. Paint the sun rays with Lemon Custard.
5. Paint a thin line with Yellow Ochre next to each Lemon Custard sun ray.

Grass:
1. Basecoat the grass with Fresh Foliage.
2. Float the top of the grass with Green Forest.
3. Paint the blades of grass with Green Forest.

Cloud:
1. Paint the cloud with a 50/50 mix of Wicker White + Calypso Sky.
2. Float the outer edges of the cloud with a 50/50 mix of Calypso Sky + clear medium.

Balloons:
See the Balloon Painting Worksheet.
1. Paint one balloon with Calypso Sky. Float its bottom edge with Azure Blue.
2. Paint one balloon with Baby Pink. Float its bottom edge with Magenta.
3. Paint one balloon with Purple Lilac. Float its bottom edge with Violet Pansy.
4. Paint one balloon with Fresh Foliage. Float its bottom edge with Green Forest.
5. Float the top edges of all balloons with Wicker White.
6. Paint a Wicker White highlight in the top right curve of each balloon.

Lettering & Balloon Strings:

1. When the paint is dry, transfer the lettering to the heart.
2. Trace the letters for the name and birth date from the alphabet pattern. Transfer to the cloud.
3. Using the tip pen with Licorice, paint the balloon strings and the lettering on the heart and the cloud.

FINISH

1. Follow the manufacturer's instructions for baking or drying.
2. Tie the yellow ribbon into a bow and glue it over the pig's ear. ❑

BALLOONS PAINTING WORKSHEET

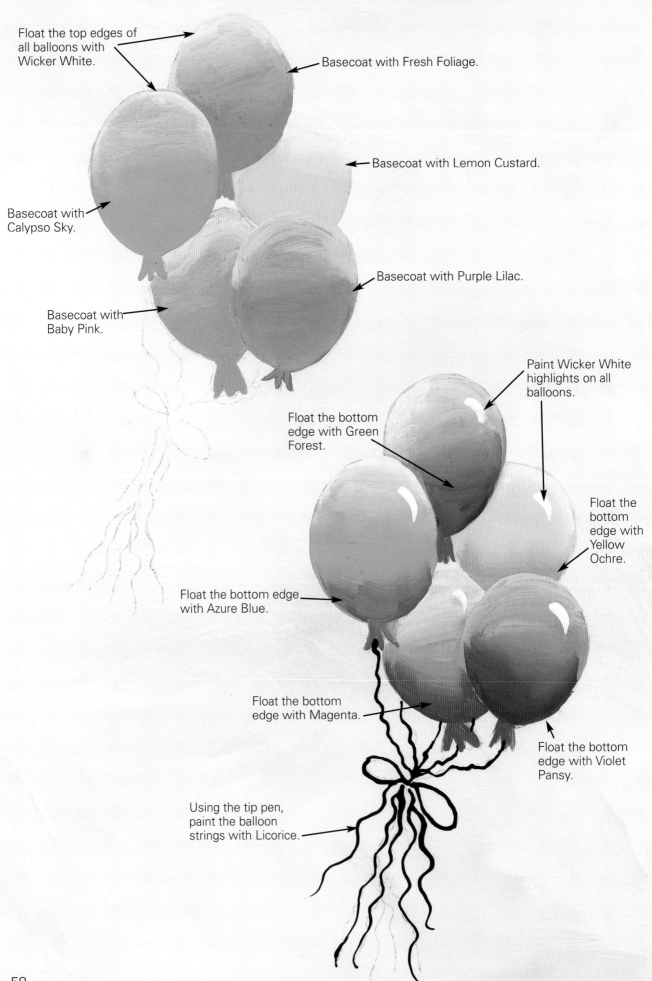

Float the top edges of all balloons with Wicker White.

Basecoat with Fresh Foliage.

Basecoat with Lemon Custard.

Basecoat with Calypso Sky.

Basecoat with Purple Lilac.

Basecoat with Baby Pink.

Paint Wicker White highlights on all balloons.

Float the bottom edge with Green Forest.

Float the bottom edge with Yellow Ochre.

Float the bottom edge with Azure Blue.

Float the bottom edge with Magenta.

Float the bottom edge with Violet Pansy.

Using the tip pen, paint the balloon strings with Licorice.

Pattern for Welcome Baby Piggy Bank
Enlarge patterns 110% for actual size

Alphabet for Welcome Baby Piggy Bank

Pattern for Basket of Fruit Tiles
Enlarge patterns 150% for actual size

Basket of Fruit
Framed Tiles

I used a glossy paint to produce extra-juicy colors for the fruit and foliage on these tiles. They look great in a frame on the wall, and they could also be used as a cold trivet.

SUPPLIES

Acrylic Enamel Colors:

Black

Blue Purple

Brown

Golden Brown

Green

Magenta

Maroon

Orange

Pine Green

Purple

Red

Red Purple

White

Yellow

Surfaces:

Four glazed ceramic tiles, 6"
    x 6"

Brushes:

Round - #2, #4

Angular - ¼", ½"

Liner - 2/0, #2

Other Supplies:

Clear medium

Rubbing alcohol

Tracing paper

Transfer paper

Glue for mosaics

Grout mix

Wood frame, 12" x 12", to
    hold four tiles

PREPARATION

1. Clean the tile surfaces with rubbing alcohol.
2. Trace the pattern and transfer the design.

PAINT THE DESIGN

Basket:
1. Basecoat the basket weave segments with Golden Brown.
2. Float the bottom edges of the segments with Brown.
3. Thin Golden Brown with Clear Medium and use the ½" angular brush to paint the surface under the basket.
4. Shade the surface just under the basket using the same brush with thinned Brown.

Bow:
1. Basecoat the bow with Red Purple.
2. Float the bottom edges with Maroon.
3. Float the top edges with White.
4. Paint the lines with White.

Grapes:
1. Basecoat the grapes with a 50/50 mix of Blue Purple + Red Purple.
2. Float the bottom edges of the grapes with Purple.
3. Paint a White highlight on each grape.
4. Basecoat the grape leaf with Green.
5. Float the outer edges of the leaf with Pine Green.
6. Blend a little Yellow into the center of the leaf.
7. Paint tendrils with the #2 round brush using Brown.

Watermelon:
1. Basecoat the watermelon with Magenta.
2. Float the top of the watermelon with White.
3. Paint the seeds with Black.
4. Paint a White highlight in each seed.
5. Basecoat the watermelon rind with Green.
6. Float the outer curve of the rind with Pine Green.
7. Create the shadow under the bow with an additional float of Pine Green.

Cherries:
1. Basecoat the cherries with Red.
2. Float the bottom edges of the cherries with Maroon.
3. Paint the stems with Green.
4. Basecoat the leaves with Green.
5. Blend Yellow onto the tips of the leaves.
6. Float Pine Green at the stem end of each leaf.
7. Paint the leaf veins with Pine Green.

Pineapple:
1. Basecoat the pineapple sections with Golden Brown.
2. Float the bottom of each section with Brown.
3. Basecoat the pineapple leaves with Green.
4. Float the bottom edges of the leaves with Pine Green.
5. Blend Yellow at the tips of the leaves.

Orange:
1. Basecoat the orange with Orange.
2. Paint the stem hole with Brown.

Border:
1. Paint the wavy line with Purple.
2. Add White highlights in this Purple line.
3. Paint the circles on both sides of the Purple line with Green.
4. Paint a Red Purple dot in the center of each circle.

FINISH

1. Let the paint dry at room temperature for 24 hours. Keep the tiles horizontal until they are thoroughly dry, as the colors may slide on non-porous surfaces.
2. Follow the paint manufacturer's instructions for baking and cooling.
3. Glue the tiles to the backboard of the frame. Let the glue dry.
4. Following the grout manufacturer's instructions, apply grout between the tiles, being careful to get as little grout on the tiles as possible. Wipe away excess grout.
5. Mount the tiles in the frame when the grout is completely dry. ❑

St. Patrick's Day
Lucky Plate

SUPPLIES

Acrylic Enamel Colors:
Fresh Foliage
Green Forest
Licorice
Wicker White

Surface:
Clear glass plate, 10"

Brushes:
Round - #2
Angular - ¼"

Other Supplies:
Rubbing alcohol
Tracing paper
Blue painters tape
Tip Pen set
Flow medium
Clear medium

I believe it is even luckier to give than to receive, and it is certainly more fun to paint these shamrocks. The paint is on the back of the plate, so you can pile as many goodies as you like on the front.

PREPARATION

1. Clean the glass surface with rubbing alcohol.
2. Trace the pattern, repeating the shamrock, words, and squiggles randomly to fill the area of the plate.
3. Tape the tracing to the front of the plate. Turn the plate over. You will be able to see the design through the tracing paper from the back of the plate. Note that the lettering will read backwards from the back side of the plate.

PAINT THE DESIGN

Paint on the back side of the plate.
1. Outline all of the designs and all of the lettering using the tip pen and Licorice. Let dry completely.
2. Staying within the black outline, float the edges of the shamrock with Green Forest.
3. Paint dots in the shamrock with Wicker White. Let dry completely.
4. Paint over the entire shamrock with Fresh Foliage. Let dry completely.

FINISH

Follow the manufacturer's instructions for baking or drying. Turn the plate over and enjoy the design. ❏

Pattern

Place motifs randomly on plate

Happy Mother's Day

Plate

SUPPLIES

Acrylic Enamel Colors:

Azure Blue

Butler Magenta

Calypso Sky

Engine Red

Fresh Foliage

Fuchsia

Green Forest

Licorice

Purple Lilac

School Bus Yellow

Violet Pansy

Surface:

Clear glass plate, 10"

Brushes:

Round - #4

Angular - ¼"

Liner - #2

Other Supplies:

Rubbing alcohol

Tracing paper

Blue painters tape

Tip Pen set

Flow medium

Clear medium

This blooms-and-butterfly plate is easy to paint and looks great. The spotted ladybug adds a whimsical note to this Mother's Day gift.

PREPARATION

1. Clean the glass surface with rubbing alcohol.
2. Trace the pattern.
3. Tape the tracing to the front of the plate. Turn the plate over. You will be able to see the design through the tracing paper from the back of the plate. Note that the lettering will read backwards from the back side of the plate.

PAINT THE DESIGN

Paint on the back side of the plate.

Outlines & Lettering:
Outline the designs and lettering using the tip pen with Licorice. Let dry completely.

Roses:
1. Staying within the black outline, float one side of the swirled edge of the rose with Fuchsia. Let dry.
2. Paint the entire area of the rose with Butler Magenta.

Leaves:
1. Staying within the black outline, float one side of the leaves with Green Forest.
2. Float the other side of the leaves with School Bus Yellow. Let dry.
3. Paint the entire area of each leaf with Fresh Foliage.

Petal Flowers:
1. Float the tips of the petals with Violet Pansy.
2. Paint wavy lines the length of each petal with Violet Pansy. Let dry.
3. Staying within the black outline, paint the entire area of each petal with Purple Lilac.
4. Paint the dots in the flower centers with School Bus Yellow.

Butterfly:
1. Staying within the black outline, float the outer edges of the butterfly wings with Azure Blue. Let dry.
2. Paint the entire area of the butterfly wings with Calypso Sky.
3. Paint the butterfly body with School Bus Yellow.

Ladybug:
1. Paint the ladybug's head with Licorice.
2. Paint the ladybug's body with Engine Red. Let dry.

FINISH

Follow the manufacturer's instructions for baking or drying. Turn the plate over and enjoy the design. ❏

Pattern for Happy Mother's Day Plate
Enlarge patterns 110% for actual size

Pattern for Butterfly Garden Vase
Enlarge patterns 160% for actual size

Butterfly Garden
Vase

SUPPLIES

Acrylic Enamel Colors:
Baby Pink
Burnt Sienna
Fresh Foliage
Green Forest
Hauser Green Medium
Lemon Custard
Licorice
Magenta
Purple Lilac
Violet Pansy
Wicker White
Yellow Ochre

Surface:
Glass vase, 15"

Brushes:
Angular - ⅛", ¼"
Round - #2, #4
Script liner - 2/0
Liner - #2

Other Supplies:
Clear Medium
Flow Medium
Tracing paper
White transfer paper
Rubbing alcohol

There is nothing more delightful than receiving a bouquet of beautiful flowers. But even better is receiving them in a hand painted vase.

PREPARATION

1. Clean the glass surface with rubbing alcohol.
2. Trace the design on to tracing paper. Trace over the design to transfer the design to the surface using white transfer paper.

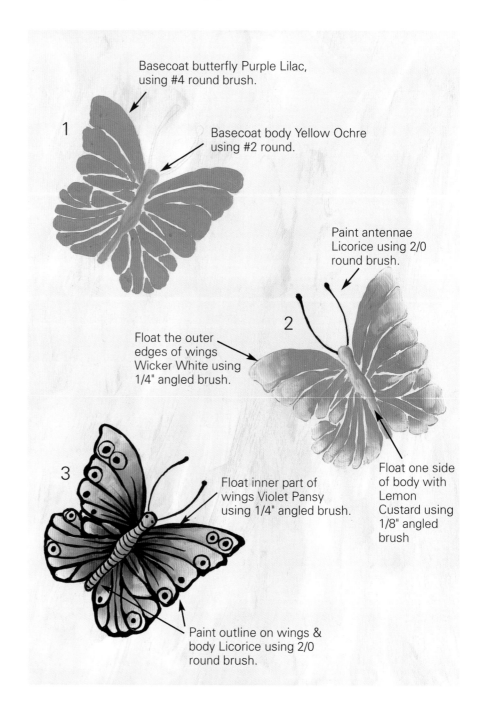

Basecoat butterfly Purple Lilac, using #4 round brush.

Basecoat body Yellow Ochre using #2 round.

Paint antennae Licorice using 2/0 round brush.

Float the outer edges of wings Wicker White using 1/4" angled brush.

Float one side of body with Lemon Custard using 1/8" angled brush

Float inner part of wings Violet Pansy using 1/4" angled brush.

Paint outline on wings & body Licorice using 2/0 round brush.

PAINT THE DESIGN

Butterfly:
1. Basecoat the butterfly with Purple Lilac using a #4 round brush.
2. Float the inside of the wings closest to the body with Violet Pansy using a ¼" angular brush.
3. Float the outer edges of the wings Wicker White using a ¼" angular brush.
4. Basecoat the butterfly body Yellow Ochre using a #2 round brush. Float one side of the body Lemon Custard using a ⅛" angular brush.
5. Paint the outline & detail on the wings, body and antennae Licorice using a #2/0 script liner brush.

Leaves:
1. Basecoat the larger leaves Fresh Foliage using a #4 round brush.
2. Paint the vein down the center of the leaves Green Forest using a #2 liner brush.
3. Float on each side of the Green Forest vein in the center of the leaves with Hauser Green Medium using a ¼" angular brush.
4. Float the outer edge of the leaves Lemon Custard using a ¼" angular brush.
5. Paint the veins in the leaves Green Forest using a #2 liner brush.

Ferns:
1. Basecoat the fern leaves & stems Burnt Sienna using a #2 round brush.
2. Paint the centers of the fern leaves Yellow Ochre using a #2 round brush.
3. Paint a highlight at the base of the leaves (on top of the Yellow Ochre) Lemon Custard using a 2/0 script liner brush.

Flowers:
1. Basecoat the flowers Magenta using a #2 round brush. While the paint is still wet paint the inside of the petals using a 2/0 script liner brush with Baby Pink - blending the paint slightly.
2. Paint the centers of the flowers Lemon Custard using a 2/0 script liner brush.

Swirls:
Paint the large swirls with a 50/50 mix of Fresh Foliage and Lemon Custard using a #2 liner brush.

FINISH

1. To acquire a glossy finish that will help to seal the design, paint one coat of Clear Medium over the entire design.
2. Follow manufacturer's instructions on paint bottle for baking and drying paints. ❏

Happy Father's Day
Martini Glasses

SUPPLIES

Acrylic Enamel Colors:
Licorice
Wicker White
Fresh Foliage
Thicket
Engine Red
Berry Wine

Surface:
Clear glass martini glasses

Brushes:
Angular - ⅛", ¼"
Round - #4
Script liner - #2/0
Liner #2
Flat - #4

Other Supplies:
Clear Medium
Flow Medium
Rubbing Alcohol
Tracing Paper

Show dad your appreciation and that you approve of his wicked ways.

PREPARATION

1. Clean glasses with rubbing alcohol.
2. Transfer the design to tracing paper. Tape the olives/pattern to the inside of the glass.

PAINT THE DESIGN

1. Paint the stem Licorice using a #4 round brush. Let dry.
2. Paint the checks at the bottom of the glass and at the rim with Licorice and Wicker White (alternating colors) using a #4 flat brush.
3. Paint the lines coming up from the center of the glass/stem Wicker White using a #2 liner brush.
4. Paint the dots at the top of these Wicker White lines Licorice using a 2/0 script liner. Let dry.

Olives:
1. Basecoat the olives Fresh Foliage using a #2 round.
2. Float the bottom edge of the olives with Thicket using a ¼" angular brush.
3. Paint the pimiento in the olives Engine Red using a #2 round. Float the bottom edge of the pimiento with Berry Wine using a ⅛" angular brush.

FINISH

1. To acquire a glossy finish that will help to seal the design, paint one coat of Clear Medium over the entire design.
2. Follow manufacturer's instructions on paint bottle for baking and drying paints. ❏

Enlarge patterns 180% for actual size

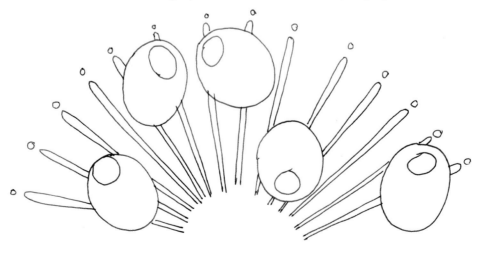

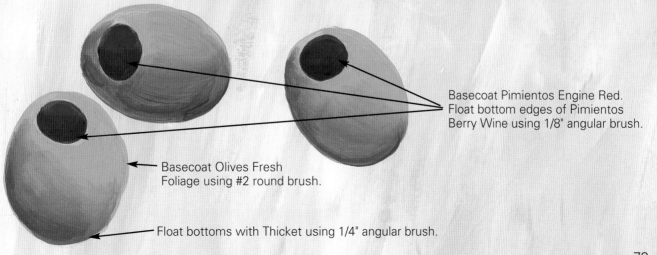

Basecoat Pimientos Engine Red.
Float bottom edges of Pimientos
Berry Wine using 1/8" angular brush.

Basecoat Olives Fresh
Foliage using #2 round brush.

Float bottoms with Thicket using 1/4" angular brush.

Pretty in Blue
Vase

The rose and foliage colors look more vivid in contrast with the deep blue glass of this vase. Create the trellis pattern with carefully placed masking tape.

SUPPLIES

Acrylic Enamel Colors:
Baby Pink
Berry Wine
Burnt Sienna
Fresh Foliage
Green Forest
Lemon Custard
Magenta
Wicker White

Surface:
Blue glass vase, 11" tall

Brushes:
Round - #2, #4
Angular - ⅛", ¼", ½"
Liner - #2
Script liner - 0

Other Supplies:
Rubbing alcohol
Tracing paper
Transfer paper
Painter's masking tape or grout tape, ⅜"
Sea sponge
Flow medium
Clear medium

PREPARATION

1. Clean the glass surface with rubbing alcohol.
2. Using the ⅜" painters masking tape, tape horizontally just below the top rim of the vase. Space down about 1" and place another piece of tape horizontally around the neck of the vase. Repeat one more time about 1" down.
3. Place pieces of tape vertically about 1" apart around the neck of the vase. It will look like a checkered pattern.
4. Place three rows of tape horizontally around the middle of the vase, about 1" apart. Place vertical strips of tape about 1" apart around the middle of the vase.
5. Using a small sea sponge, sponge Wicker White over the two areas of tape, overlapping the edges of the tape. Let dry. Remove the tape.
6. Trace the pattern and transfer the design to the vase.

PAINT THE DESIGN

Roses:
See the Roses Painting Worksheet.
1. Basecoat the roses with Baby Pink.
2. Float the bottom edges of the roses with Magenta.
3. Paint the centers of the roses with Magenta.
4. Float the bottom edges of the centers with Berry Wine.
5. Paint the swirls around the centers with Magenta.
6. Paint the dots in the centers of the roses with a 50/50 mix of Wicker White + Baby Pink.

Leaves:
See the Roses Painting Worksheet.
1. Basecoat the leaves with Fresh Foliage.
2. Float the bottom edges of the leaves with Green Forest.
3. Float the top edges of the leaves with Lemon Custard.
4. Paint the leaf veins with Green Forest.
5. Paint the dots around the outside of the leaves with Wicker White.

Bow:
1. Basecoat the bow with Lemon Custard.
2. Float the bottom edge of the bow with Burnt Sienna.
3. Float the top edge of the bow with Wicker White.
4. Paint the vertical lines throughout the bow with Burnt Sienna.

FINISH

Follow the manufacturer's instructions for baking or drying. ❑

ROSES PAINTING WORKSHEET

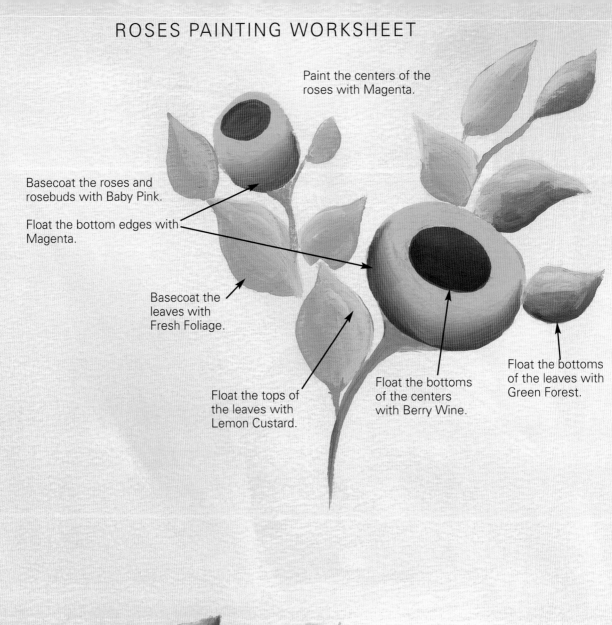

Paint the centers of the roses with Magenta.

Basecoat the roses and rosebuds with Baby Pink.

Float the bottom edges with Magenta.

Basecoat the leaves with Fresh Foliage.

Float the tops of the leaves with Lemon Custard.

Float the bottoms of the centers with Berry Wine.

Float the bottoms of the leaves with Green Forest.

Paint the leaf veins with Green Forest.

Paint the swirly lines in the roses with Berry Wine.

Paint the dots in the centers with a 50/50 mix of Wicker White and Baby Pink.

Pattern for Pretty in Blue Vase
Enlarge patterns 133% for actual size

Cinco de Mayo
Glassware Set

SUPPLIES

Transparent Glass & Ceramic Paints:

Amaranthine (Purple)

Bengal Pink

Lemon

Orange

Pepper Red

Saffron Yellow

Turquoise

Gold Outliner *(in a tube)*

Surfaces:

Margarita glasses, clear,
7-½" tall x 4½" diameter

Clear glass candy bowl,
4" tall x 7" diameter

Brushes:

Round - #4

Other Supplies:

Painter's masking tape or grout
tape, ¼"

Note: These festive glasses are painted all the way to the rim. Check the label of your transparent glass paint to be certain the brand you are using is food safe.

No drawing and measuring are needed; simply use masking tape to create sparkling stripes of clear glass to separate these brilliant transparent colors. Paint the base of each glass a different color.

PREPARATION

1. Clean the glass surfaces with rubbing alcohol.
2. Referring to the photo, apply strips of tape vertically to each glass, from rim to stem. Space the strips about 1" apart at the rim. The area between the strips of tape is wide at the rim and narrows to a point at the stem.
3. Referring to the photo, apply strips of tape vertically to the bowl, spaced about 1" apart at the rim. The area between the strips of tape is wider at the rim and narrower at the base of the bowl.

PAINT THE DESIGN

1. Paint the stripes around the glasses and bowl, alternating the colors as follows: Lemon, Saffron Yellow, Orange, Pepper Red, Bengal Pink, Amaranthine, Turquoise. Let dry and remove the tape.
2. Using the Gold Outliner, squeeze out tiny dots along the edges of the painted areas.
3. Paint the bases of the glasses with different colors of your choice. Let dry.
4. Squeeze out the swirl design with the Gold Outliner on the bases of the glasses. Let dry.

FINISH

Follow the manufacturer's instructions for baking. ❏

Pattern for Bases of
Margarita Glasses

Happily Ever After
Frame & Toast Glasses

SUPPLIES

Acrylic Enamel Colors:
Frost White
Licorice
Wicker White

Surface:
Scrapbook or album frame,
   12" x 12"
Champagne flutes, 9" tall

Brushes:
Flat - ⅛", ¼", #6

Other Supplies:
Rubbing alcohol
Tracing paper
Blue painters tape, 1"
Tip Pen set
Adhesive clear rhinestones, ¼"
"Happily Ever After" photo,
   5" x 7", your choice
Scrapbook paper, 12" x 12",
   1 sheet, your choice of color
Decorative ribbon

Make their wedding day even more memorable with monogrammed champagne flutes for the bride and groom and a personalized frame for their most romantic photo. Create the frosted effect of etched glass with paint and add sparkle with clear rhinestones.

PREPARATION

1. Remove the glass from the frame. Clean the surfaces of the glass and the champagne flutes with rubbing alcohol.
2. Trace the pattern. I have included a pattern for the entire alphabet of my style of letters so that you may personalize the names at the bottom of your frame and the initials on the champagne flutes.
3. Place tape from top to bottom, 2" in from each side of the glass from the frame.
4. Apply tape to mask a 1" wide band around the rim of each champagne flute, and another 1" wide area at the bottom of the bowl of each champagne flute.

PAINT THE DESIGN

Frame:
1. Paint the 2" strips on the right and left of the glass with Frost White. Let dry.
2. Tape the traced pattern behind the glass.
3. Basecoat the birds, bow, and leaves with Wicker White.
4. With a light gray mix of 3 parts Wicker White + 1 part Licorice, float the bottom edges of the birds and leaves.
5. Add a touch more Licorice to the mix. Paint the line under the bird bodies, bird wings, leaves, bow, lines in the birds' tails, and veins in the leaves.
6. Paint the dots in the birds' eyes with Licorice.
7. Using the tip pen with Wicker White, paint the vines, stars, letters, and the scallop & dot borders at the edges of the Frost White areas.

Champagne Flutes:
1. Paint the area between the masking tape with Frost White. Let dry.
2. Tape the traced monogram letter inside the champagne flute.
3. Using the tip pen with Wicker White, paint the letter and the scallop & dot borders around the top and bottom edges of the Frost White band.
4. Paint Wicker White scallops with the tip pen around the bases of the champagne flutes.
5. Paint the stems of the champagne flutes with Wicker White. Let dry.

FINISH

1. Follow the manufacturer's instructions for baking or drying.
2. Add adhesive rhinestones to accent your painted pieces.
3. Mount the photo on the scrapbook paper, and insert in the frame. I used lavender paper, which shows up nicely behind the frosted paint.
4. Tie ribbon to the stems of the champagne flutes. ❏

Pattern for the Happily Ever After Frame

Enlarge pattern 145% for actual size

Alphabet for the Happily Ever After Frame and Champagne Flutes
Enlarge patterns 133% for actual size

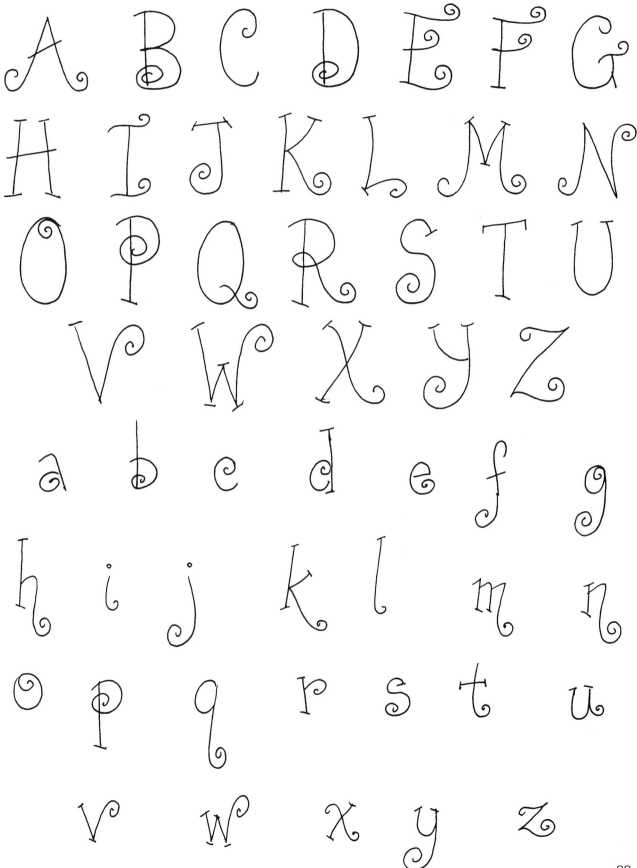

Fall Holiday

Plate

Seasons change, but these autumn leaves will remain brilliant all year. Reverse painting on a clear glass plate lets the fall colors shine through.

PREPARATION

1. Clean the glass surface with rubbing alcohol.
2. Trace the pattern, repeating the leaves, words, and squiggles to fill the area of the plate.
3. Tape the tracing to the front of the plate. Turn the plate over. You will be able to see the design through the tracing paper from the back of the plate. Note that the lettering will read backwards from the back side of the plate.

PAINT THE DESIGN

Paint on the back side of the plate.

Outlines & Lettering:
Outline the leaves, designs, and lettering using the tip pen with Licorice. Let dry completely.

Green Leaves:
1. Staying within the black outline, float one side of the leaf with Green Forest.

Pattern for Fall Holiday Plate
Repeat motifs as needed on plate.
Enlarge 133% for actual size.

2. Float the other side of the leaf with Fresh Foliage. Let dry.
3. Paint the entire area of the leaf with Evergreen.

Maple Leaf:
1. Staying within the black outline, float one side of the leaf with School Bus Yellow.
2. Float the other side of the leaf with Coffee Bean. Let dry.
3. Paint the entire area of the leaf with Pure Orange.

Oak Leaves:
1. Staying within the black outline, float one side of the

leaf with Pure Orange.
2. Float the other side of the leaf with Burnt Sienna. Let dry.
3. Paint the entire area inside the leaf with Engine Red. Let dry.

Dots & Stars:
Paint the dots and stars with colors used for the leaves.

FINISH

Follow the manufacturer's instructions for baking or drying. Turn the plate over and enjoy the design. ❑

Owl and the Moon
Candle Holder

SUPPLIES

Acrylic Enamel Colors:
Yellow Ochre
Pure Orange
Lemon Custard
Wicker White
Licorice
Purple Lilac
Green Forest
Maple Syrup
Azure Blue
Lilac Love
Burnt Sienna

Surface:
Candle vase, 13"

Brushes:
Angular - ⅛", ¼"
Round - #2, #4
Script liner - 2/0

Other Supplies:
Clear Medium
Flow Medium
Compressed sponges
Tracing paper
Rubbing alcohol
Candle

Cast an eerie shadow upon your Halloween scene with these great candleholders.
See page 90 for pattern.

PREPARATION

1. Clean surface with rubbing alcohol.
2. Cut compressed sponge into one 2" square and into one 1¼" square. Wet the compressed sponges to expand them.

PAINT THE DESIGN

Background:
1. Dip the 2" square sponge into the Purple Lilac Paint. Holding the sponge with one point of the square at the top, sponge the diamonds onto the glass surface (about midway down from the top). Repeat again, leaving about ½" in between each of the Purple Lilac stamps until you have completed the pattern all around the entire candle vase.
2. Dip the 1¼" square into the Pure Orange Paint. Stamp evenly in between the Purple Lilac stamps. Repeat the stamp evenly all around the candle vase. Let dry.
3. Trace the design to tracing paper. Place the design inside the glass container and tape into place. Tape the large leaf pattern under the base of the glass container.

Owl:
1. Basecoat the owl body with Yellow Ochre using a #4 round brush.
2. Float the bottom edge of the owl body and the wing with Burnt Sienna using the ¼" angular brush.
3. Float the top of the wing, head and a little on the body with Lemon Custard using the ¼" angular brush.
4. Paint the owl's beak with Lemon Custard.
5. Outline the beak with Burnt Sienna using a 2/0 script liner.
6. Paint the owl's feet with Maple Syrup using a 2/0 script liner.
7. Paint highlights on the feet with Yellow Ochre using the 2/0 round brush.
8. Float the top of the owl's eyelids with Lemon Custard using a ⅛" angular brush. Outline the eyelids using the 2/0 script liner and Burnt Sienna. Paint the outer part of the eyes Wicker White. Paint the eye Azure Blue and paint the iris Licorice using a 2/0 script liner. Paint the highlight in each eye with the 2/0 script liner and Wicker White. Paint the eyelashes Licorice using the 2/0 script liner.
9. Paint the lines on the owl body, wing, around eyelids, eyebrows with Burnt Sienna using the 2/0 script liner.

Tree:
1. Basecoat the tree trunk and branches Yellow Ochre using the #4 round brush.
2. Float the bottom edges of the branches and one side of the tree trunk with Burnt Sienna using the ¼" angular brush.

Leaves:
1. Bascoat the leaves Fresh Foliage using the #2 round brush.
2. Float the bottom edges of the leaves with Green Forest using the ⅛" angular brush.

3. Float the top edges of the leaves with Lemon Custard using the ⅛" angular brush.
4. Paint the veins in the leaves Green Forest using the 2/0 script liner.

Moon & Star:

1. Basecoat the moon and the star Lemon Custard using the #2 round brush.
2. Float the left side of the moon and the left side of the star Yellow Custard using the ¼" angular brush.
3. Paint the line for the moon's mouth with Yellow Ochre using the 2/0 script liner.
4. Paint the eyelashes on the moon with Licorice using the 2/0 script liner brush.
5. Paint the cap on the moon with Fresh Foliage using the #2 round brush. Float the base of the cap Green Forest using the ¼" angular brush.
6. Paint the checks on the band of the hat using the 2/0 script liner using Wicker White and Licorice, alternating the colors.

Stem of the Container:

1. Paint 1" stripes around the glass stem with Purple Lilac and Pure Orange using the #4 round and alternating the colors between the stripes.
2. Float the top edge of the Pure Orange Stripes with Lemon Custard using the ¼" angular brush.
3. Float both sides of the Purple Lilac strips Lilac Love.

FINISH

1. To acquire a glossy finish that will help to seal the design, paint one coat of Clear Medium over the entire design.
2. Follow manufacturer's instructions on paint bottle for baking and drying paints. ❑

Christmas Holiday

Plate

SUPPLIES

Acrylic Enamel Colors:
Berry Wine
Engine Red
Fresh Foliage
Green Forest
Licorice

Surface:
Clear glass plate, 10"

Brushes:
Round - #2, #4
Angular - ¼"

Other Supplies:
Rubbing alcohol
Tracing paper
Blue painters tape
Tip Pen set
Flow medium
Clear medium

This reverse-painted plate is perfect for Santa's cookies. It would be easy to reduce the pattern to the right size for a set of dessert plates, too.

PREPARATION

1. Clean the glass surfaces with rubbing alcohol.
2. Trace the pattern, repeating the holly, words, and squiggles to fill the area of the plate.
3. Tape the tracing to the front of the plate. Turn the plate over. You will be able to see the design through the tracing paper from the back of the plate. Note that the lettering will read backwards from the back side of the plate.

PAINT THE DESIGN

Paint on the back side of the plate.

Outlines & Lettering:
Outline the holly and lettering, and draw the squiggles using the tip pen with Licorice. Let dry completely.

Holly Leaves:
1. Float one side of the leaf with Green Forest. Let dry.
2. Paint the entire leaf area with Fresh Foliage.

Berries:
1. Staying within the black outline, float one side of the berry with Berry Wine. Let dry.
2. Paint the entire area of the berry with Engine Red. Let dry.

FINISH

Follow the manufacturer's instructions for baking or drying. Turn the plate over and enjoy the design. ❑

Pattern
Enlarge patterns
133% for actual size.

Repeat motifs
randomly on plate.

Pattern for Owl and the Moon Candle Holder

Enlarge at 200% for actual size

Actual size

Base

PART II

Using Kiln Fired Glazes

With all the new "paint your own" pottery shops that have popped up it should be easy for you to find a place to learn how to paint and glaze bisque ceramic pieces. These shops generally offer classes, products, and access to having your pieces kiln fired so you can create your own ceramic pieces without having to make a large investment in equipment. They also carry a wide variety of unique bisque surfaces. Your imagination can run wild with ideas to create and personalize your own fired ceramics! *It is extremely important to read the manufacturer's instructions for the handling and use of all glazes.*

I have included patterns for all the projects I designed for using kiln fired glazes, but those are not your only choices. You can easily adapt any of the patterns in this book for use with kiln fired glazes. Simply follow the procedures for transferring patterns to bisque pieces, then paint with underglazes, apply clear glaze, and fire.

Glazes

Underglaze: These are the paints used to apply the designs to the bisque pieces. As the name implies, an underglaze is formulated to be used to apply color underneath a transparent glaze. There are several types of underglaze. Some types of underglazes can be applied to greenware (unfired clay pieces) and others are made to be applied to bisque. In the projects in this book, the underglazes have been applied to already fired bisque ware surfaces. Underglazes can be manipulated much like acrylic paints. They can be thinned with water for proper painting consistency.

Glazes give the smooth, glassy surface to fired ceramics. The ingredients in glazes are silica, alumina, and flux. *Silica* is the element that forms the glass. *Alumina* is the stabilizer, and the *flux* lowers the melting temperature of silica and alumina so they can be fired in a ceramic kiln. Glazes are applied over the underglazes, as the last step before firing.

Some clear glazes are tinted light blue so that the coverage area can be seen. Allow the clear glaze to dry before firing.

General Information

Glazes and underglazes are water soluble and can be cleaned up with soap and water. Ceramic glazes may be transparent, opaque or colored. Glazes also come in several finishes: gloss, matte or satin. Glazes can be applied by brushing, dipping or pouring. When the glazes are fired, they give the bisque surfaces their glassy finish. Even when you are painting a ceramic piece that will be fired in a kiln, make sure the final glaze is food safe. When using glazes and underglazes be sure you use ones that are compatible with one another. Glazes have different firing temperatures. Be sure that the person doing the firing knows the proper temperature for firing the glazes.

Food safe, non-toxic glazes: Use only non-toxic glazes on surfaces that are going to be used for food or drink. Non-toxic glazes do not contain lead or other chemicals that are considered harmful to humans. A piece is considered to be dinnerware safe if, after firing, it does not release harmful materials above limits set by the FDA.

Toxic glazes: Use these glazes for decorative purposes ONLY. Some types of toxic glazes include crystalline glazes, metallics, crackles, and some of the brilliant red- and orange-toned colored glazes, to name just a few. Because toxic or "cautionary" glazes do contain lead or other toxic materials, these types of professional glazes should be handled with caution. They should not be used by children.

Look for professional products that include the ASTM D 4236 CAUTION seal on the label which provides information on safe handling and use. This caution seal is the chronic hazard labeling standard that is now part of the U.S. labeling law.

Glazes and underglazes have different firing temperatures. Be sure you use compatible products. Also, make sure the person doing the kiln firing knows the proper firing temperatures.

Palette of Colors

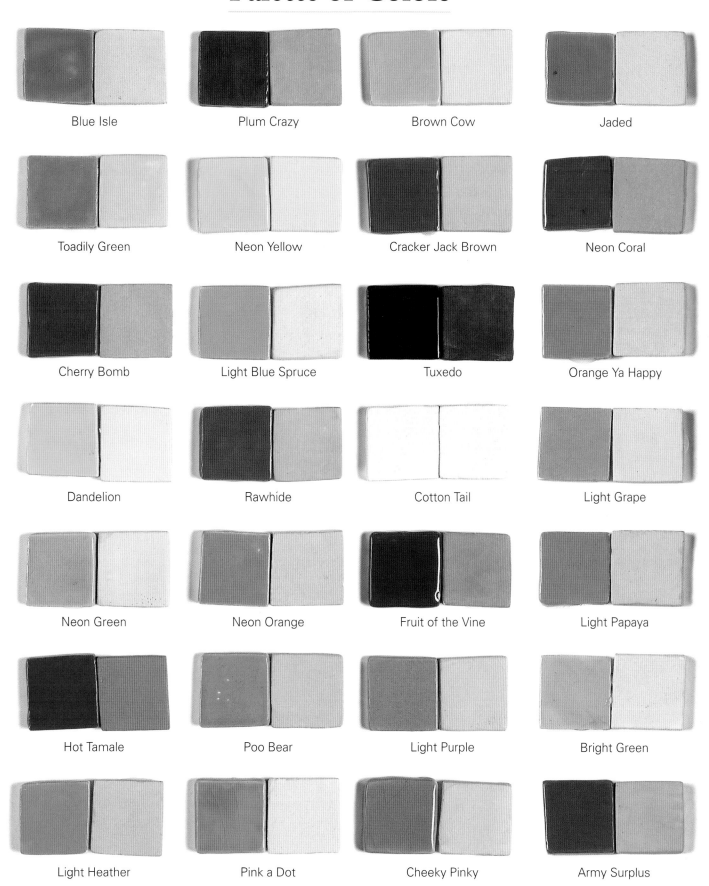

Blue Isle	Plum Crazy	Brown Cow	Jaded
Toadily Green	Neon Yellow	Cracker Jack Brown	Neon Coral
Cherry Bomb	Light Blue Spruce	Tuxedo	Orange Ya Happy
Dandelion	Rawhide	Cotton Tail	Light Grape
Neon Green	Neon Orange	Fruit of the Vine	Light Papaya
Hot Tamale	Poo Bear	Light Purple	Bright Green
Light Heather	Pink a Dot	Cheeky Pinky	Army Surplus

Brushes

See page 12 for photos of brushes.

The same brushes that are used for acrylic enamels can be used for painting glazes on bisque. Glazes and underglazes can be cleaned up with soap and water, so it is easy to keep your brushes in good condition. Use the largest size brush that feels comfortable; your goal is to fill the design area with a single stroke rather than many small strokes. Brushes come in a variety of types and sizes. The basic brushes used for the kiln fired projects in this book include:

Round: Sizes 2, 4, 6
Round brushes have a round ferrule with hairs that come to a point. They are excellent for basecoating, painting details, and small areas such as the tips on leaves and hearts.

Script Liner: Size 2/0, 2, 4
The script liner is a long-haired round brush used for detail work such as scrolls, spirals, and swirls. It is used with underglazes thinned to an ink-like consistency. To load the brush, roll the script liner into the thinned underglaze, pulling toward you. Hold the brush perpendicular to your surface and apply light pressure to paint the design.

Liner: Size 2
A liner brush has slightly shorter hairs than a script liner. The hairs come to a fine point and the brush creates delicate, slender lines that are excellent for line work, lettering, outlining, adding details and flowing lines for eyes, vines, etc. To load the brush, roll the hairs into thinned underglaze, pulling toward you. Hold the brush perpendicular to your surface and apply light pressure to paint the design.

Angular: Size ½", ¼", ⅛"
An angular brush is a flat brush that is cut at an angle. This brush is used for floating and side-loading.

Flat (Bright): - Size 6
Flats are rectangular shaped brushes that have a chisel edge. They are used for basecoating, wide stripes, and stroke leaves.

Square Wash: Size 1"
A wash brush is used for basecoating large areas or for applying glazes.

Other Tools

Sgraffito tool: "Sgraffito" refers to the technique of "scratching" a design through a top layer to reveal the color in a layer beneath. This tool has a sharp steel blade that cuts easily through a layer of underglaze. Vary the depth and thickness of the line by changing the angle and amount of pressure you apply.

Dauber
This paint applicator looks like a dowel with a small rounded sponge on one end. Daubers generally come in ¼" and ½" sizes. To use the dauber, dip the sponge in the color of your choice, offload on the palette or blot to remove excess underglaze, and dab on a nice rounded dot of color.

Sponge Applicator
The sponge applicator is a round sponge on a dowel. The painting surface of the sponge is flat rather than domed. Sponge applicators come in various sizes. To use the tool, dab the flat surface of the sponge into the color,

offload on the palette or blot to remove excess underglaze, then dab to form a uniform round dot on your surface.

Sea Sponge
Apply underglaze with a natural sea sponge for a softly textured effect. Moisten the sponge with water to soften it, then squeeze out the water so the sponge is barely damp. Dab it into the color, offload on the palette to remove excess paint, and apply to the surface in overlapping dabbing motions.

Surfaces for Painting

Think of ceramic bisque ware as the blank canvas for your creative expression-but it's three-dimensional and comes in a huge range of shapes and sizes, from casseroles to angel and elf figurines to plates, bowls, mugs, and more!

Bisque ware is readily available at "paint your own" pottery shops, and can be ordered from many on-line sources.

Bisque is a piece of dried clay that has been hardened through a first firing in a ceramic kiln at temperatures around 2000 degrees F. The clay shape and surface are hard and stable, ready to accept your decoration. At this stage, the piece can be painted with underglazes, a glaze applied, then fired.

If a piece is going to be used for decorative purposes only, it can be painted with acrylic paints and sprayed with a finish. No firing is required.

Greenware is a clay object that has dried, but has not yet been fired. Unfired greenware is very fragile. It must be fired before it can be painted and decorated.

Preparation

Bisque surfaces are ready to paint; no sanding is needed. Simply brush off any visible dust from the surface, then wipe it with a damp sponge to remove any traces of dust.

Other Supplies

For Preparing the Surface

Use a damp **soft sponge** to clean the surface of a bisque piece before you transfer the pattern and begin painting the design.

For Transferring Designs

Use **tracing paper** and a **fine point black permanent pen** or a **pencil** to trace patterns from the book.

Transfer paper is a thin paper, coated on one side with chalk or graphite, that is used for transferring designs. It comes in a variety of brands, colors, and sizes and can be purchased in large sheets, rolls, and smaller packages that have an assortment of colors.

Use a light gray graphite paper for transferring designs to bisque surfaces. These lines will be covered by the underglazes and will burn away when the piece is fired in the kiln.

A **stylus** is a tool with a small rounded tip that is used to transfer designs using transfer paper. I use a **red ballpoint pen** to transfer patterns; it's easy to see which pattern lines I have transferred.

You can also sketch on bisque with a **pencil.** Keep pencil lines as light as possible so they will burn off when the piece is fired.

For Painting

You'll need **paper towels** for blotting brushes and cleaning up your work area, a **water basin** for rinsing brushes, and **foam plates** for holding underglazes.

Painting with Glazes

For the projects in this book, I have applied underglazes to bisque surfaces that have already been fired once. Underglazes dry to a soft, chalk-like finish. Colors are light in intensity until they have been fired.

Applying an Underglaze

1. First clean the surface with a damp sponge to remove any dust.
2. Brush on one coat of underglaze with a good quality, soft brush, then apply a second coat diagonally over the first coat to achieve good coverage. Bisque is porous and absorbs the underglaze quickly, so paint smoothly and use as few brush strokes as possible. Allow the second coat of underglaze to dry.
3. Apply the transparent glaze and fire the piece in the kiln. Underglaze colors become brilliant when they have been fired under a clear glaze.

Applying Glaze

Glazes can be applied by several different methods. Make sure the bisque piece is clean and free of dust particles by wiping the surface with a clean damp sponge.

Dipping Glaze Method

Pour the glaze into a clean container and mix well. *Note: Make sure you have a large enough container and enough glaze to submerge your bisque piece.* Dip one-half to two-thirds of the bisque piece into the glaze and quickly lift it out. Turn the piece over and dip the remainder of the

piece into the glaze, overlapping the edges slightly. You can touch up any missed areas with a brush.

Brush-on Method

Simply dip a brush into the glaze and brush glaze onto the surface of the bisque piece. Bisque absorbs the glaze quickly, as it is very porous, so brush it on as smoothly as possible. Allow the first layer of glaze to dry before brushing on a second coat. Depending on the brand of glaze, a third coat may be recommended. Read the specific directions on the glaze to determine the number of coats necessary.

Pouring Method

Pouring is done when bisque surfaces are too large to dip. Pour glaze over the surface of the bisque, covering the inside and outside of the piece. Allow the first coat of glaze to dry. Pour a second coat of glaze over the bisque, smoothing any drips with a soft brush.

Firing the Glazes

Firing is the process of baking a ceramic piece, either greenware or bisque, in a ceramic kiln in order to harden it or heat the glaze to a high enough temperature so that the glaze ingredients fuse together to form a glass-like finish. Firing is done at different temperatures depending on the type of clay or glazes. Manufacturers list the recommended firing temperatures on the labels of their products.

Transferring the Designs

Using the Patterns

This book includes patterns for all the projects. Use a photocopy machine to enlarge or reduce the pattern if necessary to fit your piece. Trace the pattern onto tracing paper with a black fine point permanent pen.

Transferring the Pattern

Use a transfer paper that leaves wax-free, greaseless lines. A light gray graphite transfer paper works well on bisque surfaces.

Position the traced pattern on the surface and secure it in place with tape at the top edge. Place the transfer paper between the tracing and the surface, shiny side down. Retrace the pattern with a stylus or a ballpoint

pen to transfer it to the surface. Trace as gently as possible; you want the transferred graphite lines to be very light. There is no need to erase the transferred lines. They will be covered by underglaze or will burn off when the piece is fired.

Freehand Drawing

For a very simple design, use the pattern as a reference as you draw the design directly onto the surface with a pencil. Use very little pressure and light lines. The pencil lines will burn off when the piece is fired.

If you feel confident, paint directly on the surface without the aid of pattern lines.

Masking

Masking is the technique of covering an area of the bisque piece before it is underglazed so that paint will not get on that area. **Artist's masking fluid** is a liquid used to block out areas while you paint, leaving behind or retaining the original white color of the bisque underneath. It is made of a mixture of latex and ammonia. When it is dry, it can be removed by gently peeling it off. Don't use your best brushes for applying masking fluid, as it is quite difficult to remove the fluid from a brush.

Step 1: Paint various-sized circles of masking fluid on the bisque surface. Let dry.

Step 2: Completely cover the bisque surface with underglaze, applying it right over the masking fluid. The masking fluid will resist the underglaze. Let dry.

Step 3: Remove the masking fluid to reveal circles of unpainted white bisque. Begin painting the design.

The spiral designs on this set of ruffled dinnerware were painted over dots made by using artist's masking fluid. See page 106 for complete instructions for Ruffled Ware Table Set.

Stenciling

Stenciling is a quick and easy way to add pattern to your ceramic pieces. With stencils, patterns can be repeated easily. Use a pre-cut stencil that can be purchased at most craft & hobby stores, or cut your own stencil with a craft knife or stencil cutting tool from stencil blank material.

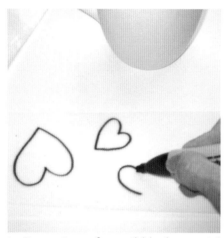

1. Cut a piece of stencil blank material to the size needed for the project you are stenciling. Draw or trace your design onto the front of the stencil blank material using a permanent marker.

This large mug, stenciled with various sizes of hearts would make a great present for a special loved one. The underglaze colors used were Dandelion, Jaded, and Neon Coral.

2. Using a craft utility knife or a stencil cutting tool, cut out the design. Use a self-healing cutting mat under the stencil blank material for best results. Tape stencil securely in place on surface.

3. Load a sponge applicator or stencil brush with your underglaze color. Pounce the color into the stencil opening. Allow underglaze to dry.

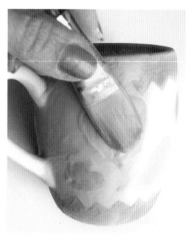

4. Using a bristle brush, apply two or three coats of clear, non-toxic glaze to entire project surface. Fire to correct temperature needed for glaze you are using.

Stamping

Stamping a design on ceramics is so much fun. There are numerous foam stamp designs available from which to choose. When using pre-cut foam stamps, apply an underglaze color to the entire surface of the stamp using a brush. Stamp it onto your palette to remove any excess paint and distribute the paint evenly on the stamp. Then press the stamp evenly on the surface. To avoid smearing the image, lift the stamp straight up.

It is also fun to cut your own stamp. You can cut a design from a compressed sponge, a cellulose sponge, foam, or even vegetables. In the following photos, you will see how an ordinary potato was used to create this fun design shown on this 11" plate.

1. Basecoat the surface of your ceramic piece with the underglaze color of your choice. Here Dandelion was used to basecoat the plate.

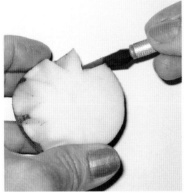

2. Using a pencil or a marker, draw a design on the flat side of a potato that has been cut in half. Use a craft utility knife to carve the design into the potato.

3. Dip the stamp into the underglaze color of your choice or apply the color to the stamp with a brush. Here Tuxedo underglaze was used on these two stylized designs. Stamp the design evenly on the surface.

4. To make the dots on this design, an eraser was dipped into the color and then stamped onto the surface. Allow underglaze to dry.

5. Brush on a coat of clear glaze over the underglaze design. Allow to dry. Fire to the temperature required for the glazes you are using.

Sponging

Great-looking texture can be quickly applied to a surface using a sea sponge or a heavily textured cellulose sponge. On this 12" diameter bowl, six underglaze colors were used to add stripes of texture. The underglaze colors used were Orange Ya Happy, Pink a Dot, Dandelion, Toadily Green, Turquoise, Light Grape, and black (Tuxedo) to make the wavy lines between the colors.

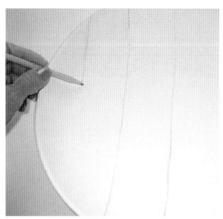

1. If you plan to have sections of texture, use a pencil to draw the areas to be sponged.

2. Start with a damp sea sponge. Dip the sponge in water and squeeze dry. Dip the sponge into the underglaze color of your choice.

3. Lightly pounce the sponge onto the surface, letting some of the background show through to get a textured effect.

4. Continue sponging until you have covered the areas you intend to be textured.

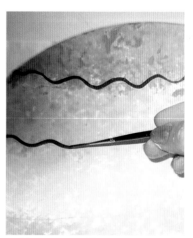

5. Here, to add contrast to the design, a liner brush was used to paint wavy lines between each of the sponged underglaze colors. Allow all colors to dry. Coat with two or three coats of a clear, non-toxic glaze. Allow to dry. Fire at the temperature required for your glaze.

Sgraffito

Sgraffito is a decorative technique in which the topmost layer on a surface is scratched or cut through, to show a design from the contrasting color underneath. I used a sgraffito ceramic tool to scratch my design into the underglaze, so the color below would show through.

The inside of this 9" diameter ceramic bowl uses the same colors used for the "Colorful Sgraffito Pear Bowl" on page 112, 113.

1. Draw the design onto the surface of the bisque piece with a pencil.

2. Paint in the areas with the underglaze colors of your choice. Let dry.

3. Paint over each section of the underglaze colors with a darker or contrasting color. Let dry.

4. Using a sgrafitto tool, scratch a design into the underglazed top layer. Use a light touch so you don't scratch through the bottom layer. You want the first color to show through the scratched design areas.

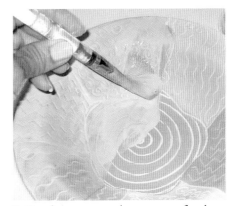

5. Brush on two to three coats of a clear, non-toxic glaze. Clear glaze appears opaque when brushed on, but turns clear with fired. Let dry. Fire to the temperature required for your glaze.

Gifty Mugs
Ceramic Mugs

Choose your message and fire your mug! Surprise a friend with a gift that will make any day a special day.

PREPARATION

1. Wipe the bisque surfaces with a damp sponge to remove all traces of dust.
2. Trace the patterns.

PAINT THE DESIGN

Base Colors:

1. Basecoat the mugs with one each of the following colors: Pink A Dot, Neon Orange, Light Blue Spruce, Light Purple, Neon Green, Neon Yellow.
2. Allow the underglazes to dry. Fire the mugs.

Sgraffito Designs:

1. Transfer the pattern outlines.
2. Paint the design area on each mug with Tuxedo. Let dry.
3. Transfer the pattern details.
4. Using the sgraffito tool, scratch the design and lettering lightly into the Tuxedo underglaze, revealing the colors below.

FINISH

Paint the mugs with clear, food safe glaze and kiln fire. ❑

SUPPLIES

Underglaze Colors:

Light Blue Spruce
Light Purple
Neon Green
Neon Orange
Neon Yellow
Pink a Dot
Tuxedo

Surfaces:

Ceramic bisque mugs, 3¾" tall x 3" diameter

Brushes:

Round - #4
Flat - #6

Other Supplies:

Sponge
Tracing paper
Transfer paper
Sgraffito tool
Clear, food safe glaze

Enlarge at 133% for actual size

Patterns for Gifty Mugs

Enlarge at 133% for actual size

Patterns for Gifty Mugs

Enlarge at 133% for actual size

Pattern for Ruffled Ware Table Set

Enlarge at 200% for actual size

Ruffled Ware

Table Set

SUPPLIES

Underglaze Colors:

Army Surplus

Cheeky Pinky

Poo Bear

Surfaces:

Ceramic bisque ruffled ware
design plates, mugs,
teapot, sugar and creamer

Other Supplies:

Sponge

Artist's masking fluid

The secret for making these spots and dots is artist's masking fluid.
The swirled floral shapes complement the ruffled edges of this unusual
dinnerware set.

See page 97 showing step by step photos for masking technique.

PREPARATION

1. Wipe the bisque surfaces with a damp sponge to remove all traces of dust.
2. Paint various size circles over the entire surface using artist's masking fluid,
   leaving space between the circles. Refer to the pattern if necessary. Let the
   masking fluid dry.

PAINT THE DESIGN

1. Paint over the entire piece with Poo Bear. The areas painted with masking fluid
   will resist the underglaze. Let dry.
2. Peel off the circles of masking fluid. The circular areas that were under the
   masking fluid will remain the original white color of the bisque.
3. Paint the swirl designs inside the white circles with Cheeky Pinky.
4. Paint the leaves with Army Surplus. Let dry.

FINISH

Paint the entire piece with clear, food safe glaze and kiln fire. ❑

Trinket Dish Gifts

Small Ceramic Bowls

SUPPLIES

Underglaze Colors:
Light Blue Spruce
Light Purple
Neon Green
Neon Orange
Neon Yellow
Pink A Dot
Tuxedo

Surfaces:
Small ceramic bisque bowls,
    1¾" tall x 5¼" diameter

Brushes:
Round - #4
Flat - #6

Other Supplies:
Sponge
Tracing paper
Transfer paper
Sgraffito tool
Clear, food safe glaze

Use the sgraffito technique to give these trinket bowls their distinctive hand-made appeal.

PREPARATION

1. Wipe the bisque surfaces with a damp sponge to remove all traces of dust.
2. Trace the patterns.

PAINT THE DESIGN

Base Colors:
1. Basecoat the bowls with one each of the following colors: Pink A dot, Neon Orange, Light Blue Spruce, Light Purple, Neon Green, Neon Yellow.
2. Allow the underglazes to dry. Fire the bowls.

Sgraffito Designs:
1. Paint the inside of the bowls with Tuxedo.
2. Paint a checkered pattern around the edge of each bowl with Tuxedo. Let dry.
3. Transfer the patterns.
4. Using the sgraffito tool, scratch the designs and lettering lightly into the Tuxedo underglaze, revealing the colors below.

FINISH

Paint the bowls with clear, food safe glaze and kiln fire. ❑

Patterns for Trinket Dish Gifts

Enlarge at 133% for actual size

Patterns for Trinket Dish Gifts

Enlarge at 133% for actual size

Colorful Sgraffito Pear
Bowl

SUPPLIES

Underglaze Colors:
Army Surplus
Blue Isle
Cherry Bomb
Crackerjack Brown
Dandelion
Fruit of the Vine
Light Blue Spruce
Light Papaya
Light Purple
Toadily Green

Surface:
Ceramic bisque bowl,
    2½" tall x 11" diameter

Brushes:
Round - #6
Angular - ½"
Liner - #2

Other Supplies:
Sponge
Tracing paper
Transfer paper
Sgraffito tool
Clear, food safe glaze

Make this bowl a dramatic centerpiece with brilliant glazes and sgraffito textures.

PREPARATION

1. Wipe the bisque surface with a damp sponge to remove all traces of dust.
2. Trace the pattern and transfer the design.

PAINT THE DESIGN

Base Colors on Rim:
See the pattern for number guide to color blocks.
1. Paint blocks #1 and #6 with Light Blue Spruce
2. Paint blocks #2, #5 and #9 with Light Purple.
3. Paint blocks #3 and #7 with Light Papaya.
4. Paint blocks #4 and #8 with Dandelion.
5. Allow the underglazes to dry.
6. Fire the piece.

Pear:
1. Basecoat the pear with Dandelion.
2. Float the left side of the pear with Crackerjack Brown.
3. Paint the stem with Crackerjack Brown.
4. Paint the leaf with Toadily Green.
5. Float the bottom edge of the leaf with Army Surplus.
6. Float the top edge of the leaf with Dandelion.
7. Paint the area on the plate around the pear with Light Purple.
8. Float around the outside of the pear with Fruit of the Vine.

Sgraffito Designs on Rim:
1. Paint over #1 and #6 with Blue Isle.
2. Paint over #2, #5 and #9 with Fruit of the Vine.
3. Paint over #3 and #7 with Cherry Bomb.
4. Paint over #4 and #8 with Crackerjack Brown.
5. Using the sgraffito tool, scratch the pattern designs lightly into the top layer of underglaze. This will allow the underlying colors to show through.

FINISH

1. Paint the bowl with clear, food safe glaze. Allow to dry.
2. Fire the piece. ❏

113

Pattern for Colorful Sgraffito Pear Bowl

Enlarge at 155% for actual size

Pattern for Woof Dog Bowl

Enlarge at 133% for actual size

Woof
Dog Bowl

SUPPLIES

Acrylic Enamel Colors:
Brown Cow
Cotton Tail
Dandelion
Hot Tamale
Light Heather
Light Purple
Pink A Dot
Rawhide
Tuxedo

Surface:
Ceramic bisque dog food bowl,
3½" tall x 8" diameter

Brushes:
Round - #2, #4
Liner - #2

Other Supplies:
Sponge
Tracing paper
Transfer paper
Clear, food safe glaze

PREPARATION

1. Wipe the bisque surface with a damp sponge to remove all traces of dust.
2. Trace the pattern and transfer the design.

PAINT THE DESIGN

Dog:
1. Basecoat the dog with Rawhide.
2. Paint the ears and spots with Brown Cow.
3. Paint the dog's nose with Pink A Dot.
4. Paint the eyes and eyebrows with Tuxedo.
5. Paint the dog collar Hot Tamale.
6. Outline the dog with Tuxedo.

Here's a great gift for your four-legged friends!

Bones:
1. Paint the bones with Dandelion.
2. Outline the bones with Tuxedo.

Color Blocks:
1. Paint the color blocks, alternating Light Heather and Light Purple.
2. Paint the dots on the Light Heather blocks with Cotton Tail.
3. Outline the blocks with Tuxedo.

Lettering:
Paint "WOOF" lettering with Tuxedo.

Dots in Bowl:
1. Paint the dots inside the bowl with Light Heather and Light Purple.
2. Paint the swirls on the dots with Tuxedo.

FINISH

1. Paint the bowl with clear, food safe glaze and kiln fire.
2. Then…give it to the happy puppy in your house! ❏

Woof

Photo Frame

SUPPLIES

Underglaze Colors:
Brown Cow
Cotton Tail
Dandelion
Hot Tamale
Light Heather
Light Purple
Pink A Dot
Rawhide
Tuxedo

Surface:
Ceramic bisque frame, 10" wide x
    8" tall (7" x 5" opening)

Brushes:
Round - #2, #4
Liner - #2

Other Supplies:
Sponge
Tracing paper
Transfer paper
Clear glaze

PREPARATION

1. Wipe the bisque surface with a damp
   sponge to remove all traces of dust.
2. Trace the pattern and transfer the design.

PAINT THE DESIGN

Dog:
1. Basecoat the dog with Rawhide.
2. Paint the ears and spots with Brown
   Cow.
3. Paint the dog's nose with Pink A Dot.
4. Paint the eyes and eyebrows with
   Tuxedo.
5. Paint the dog collar Hot Tamale.
6. Outline the dog with Tuxedo.

The two happy puppies in this photo are my beloved dogs,
Jake and Ginger. The little guy, Jake, a long-haired red
dachshund, is the one with the big attitude! Ginger, a mutt we
got from Beagle Rescue, is the big girl, and she's a sweetheart. I
know – she doesn't look anything like a beagle. Can you tell I
am a dog lover?

Bones:
1. Paint the bones with Dandelion.
2. Outline the bones with Tuxedo.

Color Blocks:
1. Paint the color blocks, alternating Light Heather and Light Purple.
2. Paint the dots on the Light Heather blocks with Cotton Tail.
3. Outline the blocks with Tuxedo.

Lettering:
Paint "WOOF" lettering with Tuxedo.

FINISH

Glaze the frame and kiln fire. ❏

Pattern for Woof Photo Frame

Enlarge at 110% for actual size

Woof Dog Lover
Sign

SUPPLIES

Underglaze Colors:
Cotton Tail
Dandelion
Light Heather
Light Purple
Tuxedo

Surface:
Ceramic bisque sign, 5½" wide x
1½" tall (This sign comes with
the wire and the beads.)

Brushes:
Round - #2, #4
Liner - #2

Other Supplies:
Sponge
Tracing paper
Transfer paper
Clear glaze

PREPARATION

1. Remove the wire and beads.
2. Wipe the bisque surface with a damp
   sponge to remove all traces of dust.
3. Trace the pattern and transfer the design.

Make this little sign for a dog lover you know-or for yourself. It gives fair warning that dog stories will be part of every conversation on the premises.

PAINT THE DESIGN

Bone:
1. Paint the bone with Dandelion.
2. Outline the bone and paint the words "Dog Lover" with Tuxedo.

Color Blocks:
1. Paint the color blocks, alternating Light Heather and Light Purple.
2. Paint the dots on the Light Heather blocks with Cotton Tail.
3. Outline the blocks with Tuxedo.

FINISH

1. Glaze the sign and kiln fire.
2. Attach the wire and beads after firing. ❏

Cat Lover
Sign

SUPPLIES

Underglaze Colors:
Bright Green
Cotton Tail
Dandelion
Light Heather
Tuxedo

Surface:
Ceramic bisque sign, 5½"
wide x 1½" tall (This
sign comes with the wire
and the beads.)

Brushes:
Round - #2, #4
Liner - 2/0, #2

Other Supplies:
Sponge
Tracing paper
Transfer paper
Clear glaze

Same sign-different pet! Now it identifies a cat lover.

PREPARATION

1. Remove the wire and beads.
2. Wipe the bisque surface with a damp sponge to remove all traces of dust.
3. Trace the pattern and transfer the design.

PAINT THE DESIGN

1. Basecoat the fish with Dandelion.
2. Paint the color blocks, alternating Light Heather and Bright Green.
3. Paint the dots on the Light Heather blocks with Cotton Tail.
4. Outline the fish, the color blocks, and the words "Cat Lover" with Tuxedo.
   Add details to the fish.

FINISH

1. Glaze the sign and kiln fire.
2. Attach the wire and beads after firing. ❏

Meow Cat
Bowl

SUPPLIES

Underglaze Colors:
Bright Green
Cotton Tail
Dandelion
Light Heather
Pink A Dot
Plum Crazy
Tuxedo

Surface:
Ceramic bisque cat food bowl,
   3½" tall x 8" diameter

Brushes:
Round - #2, #4
Liner - 2/0, #2

Other Supplies:
Sponge
Tracing paper
Transfer paper
Clear, food safe glaze

PREPARATION

1. Wipe the bisque surface with a damp sponge to remove all traces of dust.
2. Trace the pattern and transfer the design.

PAINT THE DESIGN

Color Blocks:
1. Paint the color blocks, alternating Light Heather and Bright Green.
2. Paint the dots on the Light Heather blocks with Cotton Tail.
3. Outline the blocks with Tuxedo.

Even the most finicky cat would approve of this food bowl, and the finicky cat's person will be delighted to receive this specially-made gift.

Cat:
1. Basecoat the cat with a 50/50 mix of Tuxedo and Cotton Tail.
2. Paint the cat's nose and inside the ears with Pink A Dot.
3. Paint the cat's collar Plum Crazy.
4. Outline the cat and paint details with Tuxedo.

Fish:
1. Paint the fish with Dandelion.
2. Outline the fish and paint details with Tuxedo.

Dots in Bowl:
1. Paint the large dots inside the bowl with Light Heather.
2. Paint the smaller dots with Dandelion or Bright Green.
3. Paint the swirls on the dots with Tuxedo.

Lettering:
Paint the word "Meow" with Tuxedo.

FINISH

Paint the bowl with clear, food safe glaze and kiln fire. ❏

Meow Cat
Frame

Alley cats and pedigreed Persians look equally handsome in this ceramic frame. It's a perfect gift for your cat-loving friends.

SUPPLIES

Underglaze Colors:
Bright Green
Cotton Tail
Dandelion
Light Heather
Pink A Dot
Plum Crazy
Tuxedo

Surface:
Ceramic bisque frame, 10" wide x 8" tall (7" x 5" opening)

Brushes:
Round - #2, #4
Liner - #2

Other Supplies:
Sponge
Tracing paper
Transfer paper
Clear glaze

PREPARATION

1. Wipe the bisque surface with a damp sponge to remove all traces of dust.
2. Trace the pattern and transfer the design.

PAINT THE DESIGN

Cat:
1. Basecoat the cat with a 50/50 mix of Tuxedo and Cotton Tail.
2. Paint the cat's nose and inside the ears with Pink A Dot.
3. Paint the cat's collar Plum Crazy.

Fish:
Paint the fish with Dandelion.

Color Blocks:
1. Paint the color blocks, alternating Light Heather and Bright Green.
2. Paint the dots on the Light Heather blocks with Cotton Tail.

Lettering, Outlines & Details
1. Outline the fish, the cat, the color blocks, and the word "Meow" with Tuxedo.
2. Paint details on the fish and cat with Tuxedo.

FINISH

Glaze the frame and kiln fire. ❏

Pattern for Meow Cat Frame

Enlarge at 110% for actual size

Pattern for Meow Cat Bowl
Enlarge at 133% for actual size

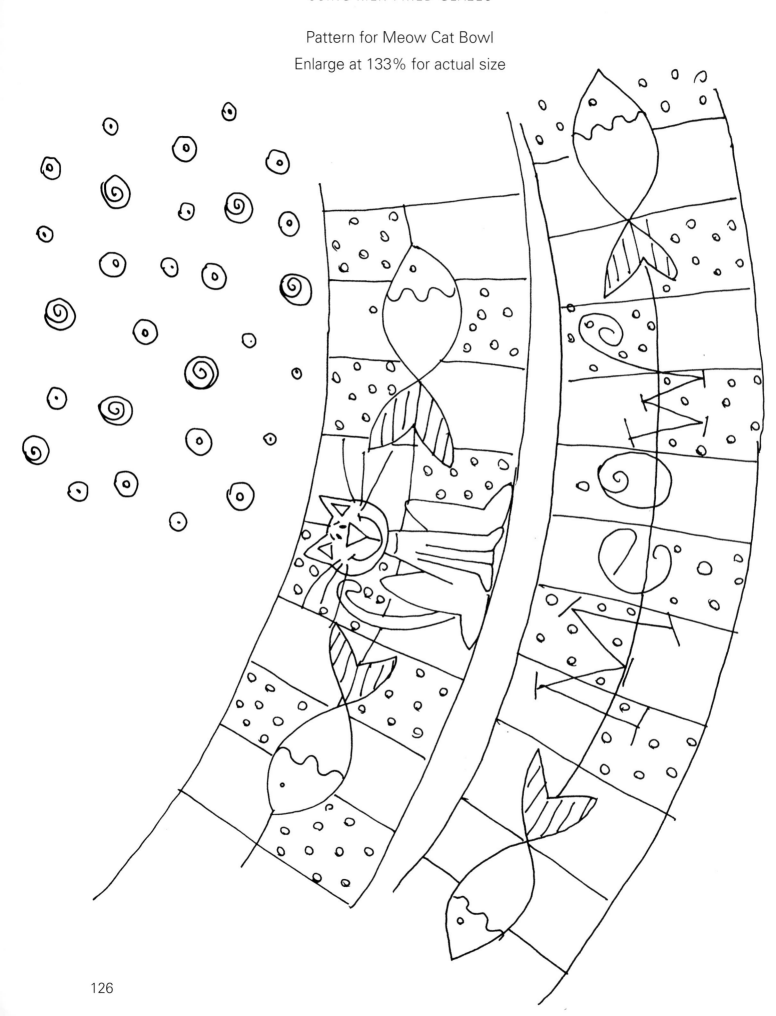

Metric Conversions

Inches to Millimeters and Centimeters

Inches	MM	CM	Inches	MM	CM
1/8	3	.3	2	51	5.1
1/4	6	.6	3	76	7.6
3/8	10	1.0	4	102	10.2
1/2	13	1.3	5	127	12.7
5/8	16	1.6	6	152	15.2
3/4	19	1.9	7	178	17.8
7/8	22	2.2	8	203	20.3
1	25	2.5	9	229	22.9
1-1/4	32	3.2	10	254	25.4
1-1/2	38	3.8	11	279	27.9
1-3/4	44	4.4	12	305	30.5

Yards to Meters

Yards	Meters	Yards	Meters
1/8	.11	3	2.74
1/4	.23	4	3.66
3/8	.34	5	4.57
1/2	.46	6	5.49
5/8	.57	7	6.40
3/4	.69	8	7.32
7/8	.80	9	8.23
1	.91	10	9.14
2	1.83		

Index

A
ABC Baby's Food Jars 50
Additional Techniques 23

B
Basket of Fruit Framed
  Ceramic Tiles 62
Bisque 95
Bloom Ceramic Mug 26
Bowl 102
  cat 122
  dog 116
Brush(es) 12, 94
  angular 12, 24, 26, 30, 34,
    36, 38, 42, 46, 50, 56,
    62, 64, 66, 70, 72, 74,
    84, 86, 88, 94, 112
  flat 12, 26, 72, 80, 94,
    104, 108
  liner 12, 30, 36, 38, 42,
    50, 56, 62, 66, 70, 72,
    74, 94, 112, 116, 118,
    120, 121, 122, 124
  round 12, 20, 24, 26, 30,
    34, 36, 38, 42, 46, 50,
    56, 62, 64, 66, 70, 72,
    74, 78, 84, 86, 88, 94,
    102, 104, 108, 112,
    116, 118, 120, 121,
    122, 124
  script liner 12, 36, 46, 70,
    72, 74, 86, 94
  square wash 12, 94
Bunny in the Garden
  Container 35, 36
Butterfly Garden Vase 70

C
Cake stand 30
Candle 86
  holder 86
Candy jar 30, 38
Canister(s) 20
Carafe 42
Cat Lover Sign 121
Cheese shaker 20
Christmas Holiday Plate 88
Cinco de Mayo Glassware
  Set 78
Citrus Delight Pitcher &
  Glasses 46
Colorful Sgraffito Pear Bowl
  112

Container 35, 36
Cotton swabs 14

D
Dauber(s) 13, 30, 94
Designs, transferring 96
Dish 108
Dream Ceramic Mug 24

E
Eraser 14

F
Fall Holiday Plate 84
Firing 96
Food Safety 9
Frame 62, 80, 118, 124
Fruit of the Vine Wine
  Glasses & Carafe 42

G
Gifty Mugs 102
Glass & Ceramic Paints 10
Glass(es) 42, 46, 72, 80
Glassware set 78

Glaze(s) 92, 102, 104, 108,
  112, 116, 118, 120, 121,
  122, 124
Glue 56, 62
Greenware 95
Grout 62, 74, 78

H
Happily Ever After Frame &
  Toast Glasses 80
Happy Father's Day Martini
  Glasses 72
Happy Mother's Day Plate 66

I
Introduction 8

J
Jar(s) 30, 38, 50

K
Kiss a Frog Candy Jar 38

L
Love Love Plate 34

Continued on next page

Index

M

Make a Wish Cake Stand & Candy Jar 30

Masking 97

    fluid 97, 106

    tape 13, 14

Meow Cat

    Bowl 122

    Frame 124

Mirror 22, 23

Miscellaneous Basic Supplies 14

Mug(s) 24, 26, 104

O

Other Supplies 95

Other Tools 13, 94

Owl & Moon Candle Holder 86

P

Paint

    acrylic enamel 10, 20, 22, 24, 26, 30, 34, 36, 38, 42, 46, 50, 56, 62, 64, 66, 70, 72, 74, 80, 84, 86, 88

    glass & ceramic 10

    medium 10, 24, 26, 34, 36, 42, 46, 50, 56, 62, 64, 66, 70, 72, 74, 84, 86, 88

    thinner 10

    transparent 10, 78

Painting

    Definitions & Techniques 17

    reverse 18

    with Glazes 96

Palette

    of colors 11, 93

    paper 14

Paper 80

    towels 14, 95

Pattern(s)

    ABC 55

basket of fruit 61

bunny in the garden 35

butterfly garden 69

bloom 27

Christmas holiday plate 88

cinco de mayo glasses 78

citrus delight 39

dream 25

fall holiday plate 84

frog 41

gifty mugs 102, 104, 105

grapes 45

happily ever after frame 82, 83

happy father's day 72

happy mother's day 68

jar lid 41

love love 33

make a wish 32

meow bowl 126

meow frame 125

owl & moon 90

pretty in blue vase (roses) 77

ruffled ware 105

sgraffito pear bowl 114

St. Patrick's Day 64

transferring 16

trinket dish gifts 110, 111

using 16

welcome baby 59, 60

woof bowl 115

woof frame 119

Pen 14, 95

    permanent 14, 95

Pencil 14, 95

Photo 80

Piggy bank 56

Pitcher 46

Plate 34, 64, 66, 84, 88

Pretty in Blue Vase 74

R

Reverse Painting 18

Rhinestones 80

Ribbon 30, 56, 80

Rubbing alcohol 14, 20, 24, 26, 30, 34, 36, 38, 42, 46, 50, 56, 62, 64, 66, 70, 72, 74, 80, 84, 86, 88

Ruffled Ware Table Set 106

S

Salt & pepper shaker(s) 20

Scissors 20

Sgraffito 101

    tool 94, 101, 102, 104, 108, 112

Sign 120, 121

Sponge applicator 13, 20, 30, 94

Sponge(s),

    compressed 86

    sea 13, 74, 94

    soft 95, 102, 104, 108, 106, 112, 116, 118, 120, 121, 122, 124

Sponging 19, 100

St. Patrick's Day Lucky Plate 64

Stamping 22, 99

Stenciling 20, 98

Stylus 14, 95

Supplies

    basic 14

    other 95

Surfaces 15, 95

T

Table set 112

Tape, painters 30, 34, 38, 42, 46, 50, 64, 66, 74, 78, 80, 84, 88

Techniques

    other 23

    painting 17

Tile(s) 15, 62

Tip pen set 13, 24, 26, 42, 56, 64, 66, 80, 84, 88

Tool(s) 13

Tracing paper 14, 20, 24, 26, 30, 34, 36, 38, 42, 46, 50, 56, 62, 64, 66, 70, 72, 74, 80, 84, 86, 88, 95, 102, 104, 108, 116, 118, 120, 121, 122, 124

Transfer paper 14, 20, 24, 26, 36, 62, 70, 74, 95, 102, 104, 108, 116, 118, 120, 121, 122, 124

Transferring Designs 96

Trinket Dish Gifts 108

Trivet 22

U

Underglaze(s) 92, 102, 104, 106, 108, 112, 116, 118, 120, 121, 122, 124

Using

    Kiln Fired Glazes 91

    Non-Fired Glass & Ceramic Paint 9

    the Patterns 16

V

Vase 69, 70, 74

W

Water basin 14, 95

Welcome Baby Piggy Bank 56

Woof Dog

    Bowl 116

    Frame 118

    Lover Sign 120

Worksheet

    apple 52

    balloons 58

    bee 52

    bloom 28

    butterfly 70

    cat 53

    duck 53

    frog 40

    grapes 44

    lemon 48

    olives 73

    party hat 29

    roses 76